WHAT IS HYPNOSIS

ABOUT THE AUTHOR

Andrew Salter has been called "the father of behavior therapy." Salter was born in Waterbury, Connecticut in 1914, and received his degree in psychology from New York University at University Heights. Professor Clark L. Hull of Yale University was responsible for launching him on his career in 1941. Salter is a consulting psychologist in New York City. His books have been translated into German, Italian, Spanish, Swedish and Japanese and acclaimed as scientific contributions. H. G. Wells, Aldous Huxley and Thomas Mann have praised his style.

OTHER BOOKS BY ANDREW SALTER

Conditioned Reflex Therapy

The Case Against Psychoanalysis

The Conditioning Therapies (WITH JOSEPH WOLPE AND L. J. REYNA)

Andrew Salter

WHAT IS HYPNOSIS

Studies in Conditioning
Including
Three Techniques of Autohypnosis

FOURTH REVISED EDITION

FARRAR, STRAUS AND GIROUX

NEW YORK

PREFACE
TO THE FOURTH REVISED EDITION

CAN we expand our minds like a balloon to which the park man has held the helium pipe? Can we control our bodies and make our organs—and the brain is an organ—dance like puppets?

"The phenomenon is surprising to the average person merely because it is rarely encountered. This, in turn, is because the particular combination of causal factors necessary to produce it rarely occurs."*

"Three Techniques of Autohypnosis" makes up Chapter Five, and has inspired many offshoots, most of them weeds which should have been plowed under. Here the reader can see the real thing.

Knowledge, they say, doubles every ten years. Not so in hypnosis. There it halves, or at least so it appears. But with a complete updating of my last chapter, "The Age of Conditioning," I have set matters straight and put a few noses out of joint. And if my conclusions make you gulp, well, they made me gulp, too.

Nevertheless, we must swallow the bitter pill of truth, and hope that it shall make us free, and not slaves.

New York City
January, 1973

---

* Said Clark L. Hull, father of scientific hypnotic research, in a related connection. HULL, C. *Hypnosis and Suggestibility.* Appleton-Century-Crofts, New York, 1933, p. 26.

PREFACE
TO THE THIRD REVISED EDITION

I HAVE written several books, but somehow this one remains my favorite. It presents an approach to hypnosis that was once quite controversial, but has since become widely accepted. New scientific ideas never kill old ones. Rather, the old ideas just fade away.

I last revised this book some nine years ago, and now, as I examine the hypnotic literature that has appeared since then, I find little reason for any further revision. In hypnosis, as elsewhere, history repeats itself. I would be remiss, however, if I did not mention the research of Theodore X. Barber. His work on the parallels between waking suggestion and hypnosis is quite significant, and firmly supports the core of this book.

Now that my thoughts about hypnosis and the conditioned reflex have become sanctified by time, I have decided to let the text stand as it is, and from here on I shall let this little book speak for itself.

New York City
October, 1963

PREFACE
TO THE FIRST EDITION

IT IS possible to answer the question "What is hypnosis?" only by considering a great number of recent experiments. It is significant that most of these have been performed by psychologists who did not realize the relevance of their findings to hypnotism. They will be bewildered to see their work considered here with mine.

This book is an effort to integrate this material, and to present for the first time a preliminary study of its basic principles, so that those engaged in hypnotic research and its applications will no longer wander on stormy seas because they have no compass.

It gives me pleasure to express my appreciation for the friendship and guidance of M. Benmosché, M.D., and W. H. Gardiner, M.D. "Three Techniques of Auto-hypnosis," now no longer available, is reprinted through the kind permission of Carl Murchison of the *Journal of General Psychology*.

I wish to thank Columbia University, the New York Academy of Medicine, and the New York Public Library for the use of their extensive collections. I am indebted to Jeannette Fahnestock, my secretary, for her always intelligent help.

Most of all I am grateful to my cases. Without their tolerant and sometimes painful coöperation I would never have acquired the insights that have resulted in this book.

New York City
April, 1943

CONTENTS

WHAT IS HYPNOSIS

CHAPTER ONE

FUNDAMENTALS: CONDITIONING AND HYPNOSIS

THE scientific method, as Julian Huxley has said, "discovers the relatedness of all things in the universe—of the motion of the moon to the influence of earth and sun, of the nature of the organism to its environment, of human civilization to the conditions under which it is made."[1]

The scientific method is naturalistic. It denies the supernatural, and declares that all phenomena are traceable to natural causes. It uses as few concepts as possible. The simplest available explanation is preferred, i.e., the one which involves the fewest or least complexly related concepts that are adequate.

When hydrogen and oxygen combine under certain conditions, water is invariably the result. Science means prediction, and prediction is the basis of control.

The schools of psychology at odds with each other give pause. Can there be a science of psychology when human behavior seems so complex that many approaches to it take refuge in deviation from naturalism? Can there be a science of psychology, when the traveler, even on the path of naturalism, staggers under a load of concepts? Can there be a science of psychology when its psychotherapy fails more often than not—in short, neither predicts nor controls, but simply does not work?

And there is surely no more unnaturalistic aspect of psychology than hypnosis. Nevertheless, keeping in mind the principles of scientific method, certain concepts of hypnosis will be developed here, and it will be shown that there is nothing puzzling about hypnosis. Rather, it will be shown that hypnosis is an aspect of the conditioned reflex, probably the most undeniable fact of modern psychology.

Pavlov's fundamental experiments with dogs are well established.[2] He found that when a hungry dog was given a piece of meat immediately after a bell was rung, and when this association of bell and meat was repeated often enough, before long the bell alone would produce a flow of saliva in the dog. It was as if the bell were acting as the meat. He called this a conditioned reflex, but "associative reflex" might be a more felicitous term. When the bell rang the dog did more than salivate. He pricked up his ears, turned his head toward the source of the food, and made anticipatory chewing movements. Pavlov, however, centered his work on a study of the salivary responses because they could be measured.

Conditioned reflexes in dogs—and what is more to the point, in *human beings*—do not involve volitional thinking. Once the conditioned reflex is trained into the subject of the experiment, he becomes a pure automaton to the non-genuine stimulus that has been woven into the reflex.

It is possible to condition other neurological mechanisms besides the salivary reflex. We know that when light shines into the pupil, it contracts, and when the light is removed, it dilates. The pupillary reflex is completely involuntary. The subject has absolutely no control over it.

There is a very significant and splendidly constructed experiment reported by C. V. Hudgins, who followed Pavlov's method, except that he conditioned the human pupillary reflex.[3] Hudgins' procedure is worth following carefully.

The pupil was first conditioned to a bell with the light as the unconditioned stimulus. Each time that this light was lit while the subject looked at it, the experimenter closed an electric circuit which rang a bell. Notice the parallel to Pavlov. The light made the pupil contract every time, and the meat made the dog salivate every time. The bell in each case was then tied to the genuine arouser of the reflex.

The subject was next taught to use his own hand-grip to close the bell and light circuits, for the more the organism is involved, the more is conditioning facilitated. The subject, then, through his own muscular activity turned on both the light and the bell. When the subject relaxed his hand at the experimenter's command, "relax," the same circuits were broken and the light would go out and the bell would stop ringing. Before long the bell and hand reactions were eliminated.

In several hours of training, Hudgins found he could omit the bell, the hand-grip, and the light. *The sound of the word "contract," spoken by him had acquired the "power" to force an involuntary and substantial contraction of the pupil.*

Let me repeat this. It is important. Hudgins, by merely saying the *word,* "contract," could now produce a strong contraction of the subject's pupil. Further, this conditioning, with and without retraining, lasted from fifteen to ninety days.

Let us say that I had similarly conditioned one of the pupils of the reader's eye. Every time I said "contract," whether you wished it or not, your pupil would obey. I would then bring you to an ophthalmologist. "Doctor," I would declare, "here is a splendid hypnotic subject. I control this person so thoroughly that at my command his pupil will contract, and perceptibly."

"Come now," he would say, "you know very well that pupillary contraction is involuntary. You need a light for that."

Nevertheless, when I said "contract," your pupil would obey every time, and the doctor would be perplexed. "How do you like hypnotism?" I would ask.

"It's amazing," he would answer, but his interest would diminish after I explained how, paralleling Pavlov and Hudgins, your pupil had been conditioned. "Well," he would say, "come back the next time you have some real hypnotism."

Our doctor is wrong. There, in the conditioned reflex, he had seen the essence of hypnosis. Hudgins' work on pupillary conditioning is quite important, so let us consider it further. Some of his subjects said the word "contract" *aloud* as he went through the conditioning procedure. Before long, these subjects, by merely saying the word "contract" could produce pupillary contraction, without the light or the bell.

He conditioned other objects to produce pupillary contraction by their *whispering* "contract" to themselves.

Finally, he conditioned five subjects to contract their pupils when they *thought* the word "contract," and to dilate them when they thought the word "relax." Light or bell was no longer needed. The subjects could auto-contract their pupils. Through conditioning it had been possible to build a control of that which was otherwise uncontrollable.

Let me make a relevant digression. What does a spectator see when a good subject is hypnotized? The hypnotist (unfortunate word) says, in a soporific voice, "Your eyes are so *heavy,* your body feels *so* tired. Oh, you feel so sleepy. You just want to *sleep.* Your arms are so *tired.* You feel so *heavy,*" et cetera. Soon the subject's eyes droop, they close, and he drifts off into a "trance."

Does it not seem plausible that the word "heavy" in good subjects was associated with heavy feelings, and that the repetition of the word "heavy" by the hypnotist acted as the bell of past associations of *actual* heavy feelings? In a sense then, hypnotists are persons who ring standard bells and find some dogs who were trained to salivate to them, in this instance, people who feel heavy and tired. "Behold," they say, "here is a good subject." How meaningless!

Let me demonstrate this more adequately. R. Menzies put a stencil patterned "XX" in front of a blue electric bulb.[4] The XX pattern would be illuminated, and the subjects would whisper "crosses" while looking at them. Two seconds later the right hand of the subject was immersed in ice water. Usually this combination of light and cold continued for thirty seconds.

Here were subjects being conditioned very much as Hudgins had done with the pupil. He had used a light, and associated pupillary contraction with a hand-grip and the word "contract." In this instance, a hand was stimulated by cold water, and the cold feeling was associated with a pattern of light and the word "crosses."

Although the right hand of the subject was immersed in ice water, the left hand remained dry, and to the lower left of this dry palm, the thenar eminence, was attached a sensitive temperature-recording device. It is a neurological fact that when one hand is suddenly chilled, the other will become somewhat chilled also— though not so much as the hand receiving the cold stimulation. This is believed due to a bilateral reflex action.

Menzies then took *actual charted recordings* of the fall in temperature of the *dry* hand as the other hand was chilled. He conditioned this chilling to the combined stimulus of a light and the repetition of the word "crosses."

After forty training sessions of about three minutes each, all five subjects whom he so conditioned, on looking at the light and saying the word "crosses" (and without any ice water) could *unconsciously* produce an actual physical drop in temperature of the left hand. This drop in temperature was measured and recorded. A constriction of the blood vessels, yielding a drop in temperature, had been produced by the light-vocal associative "bell." In short, conditioning can produce physical changes.

How easy to understand are the shivers that appropriate hypnotic "suggestion" of ice and snow produces in a good subject. He possesses verbally conditioned bells waiting to be rung. When they are rung, he shivers. No need for concepts of "suggestion" or faith.

What are words but the bells of conditioned reflexes? Through persistent associativities from infancy, the word "cloud" means "cloud," and in fact has a "cloud-like quality." As Watson says,

"We must dislodge the age-old belief that there is some peculiar essence in words as such. A word is just an explosive clutter of sounds made by expelling the breath over the tongue, teeth, and lips whenever we get around objects. We condition our children to make the same explosive sounds when they get around the same objects."[5]

Words are the bells of associative reflexes. Such words as "splendid," "marvelous," and "magnificent," give us an unconscious lift because we have been conditioned to that feeling in them. The words, "hot," "boiling," and "steam," have a warm quality because of their associativity. Inflection and gesture have been conditioned as intensifiers of word conditionings.

We can thus see that words are bound up with completely unconscious associative reflexes. Certain words in an appropriately trained person can produce actual bodily sensations, or more broadly, actual bodily reactions.

How convenient it would be to say that the phenomena of hypnosis are "caused" by "suggestion," but such a meaningless explanation has beset hypnotism for years. How much simpler and more meaningful it is to realize that hypnosis is based on associative reflexes that use words as the triggers of automatic reactions. Hypnosis is the production of reactions in the human organism through the use of verbal or other associative reflexes.

Hypnosis basically involves conditioned reactions and reflexes. Some people have conditionings which we can evoke to create the so-called "trance" state. In this state it is possible to give verbalisms of behavior to be carried out on the occurrence of an after-awakening "bell"— so-called post-hypnotic suggestion. Hypnosis is not the production of a state. It is the eliciting of one. But if the reflex patterns in hypnotic subjects are there at the start, and such seems to be the case, we are forced to entertain the curious conclusion that suggestion does not implant anything. But this is not so. Hypnosis takes advantage of something already there in order to implant something new.

Many humans do not have a background of appropriate conditionings in which, as in physics, sympathetic vibrations can be produced. In psychotherapy we may proceed with such persons by training into them whatever conditionings are necessary to solve their problems.

Pavlov alluded to the conditioned reflex approach to hypnosis.[6] Witness, "Speech, on account of the whole preceding life of the adult, is connected up with all the internal and external stimuli which can reach the cortex, signalling all of them and replacing all of them, and therefore it can call forth all those reactions of the organism which are normally determined by the actual stimuli themselves. We can, therefore, regard 'suggestion' as the most simple form of a typical conditioned reflex in man."

This is perfect. Yet Pavlov some lines later says, "I hope to be able to produce a phenomenon in animals analogous to 'suggestion' in man during hypnosis."

Nevertheless, this is what Pavlov did every time he

conditioned a glandular or motor reflex in his dogs, and that is what he was doing most of the time. Pavlov considered hypnosis a form of "general inhibition," parallel to sleep. Pavlov has a discussion of his concepts of hysteria, suggestion, autosuggestion, and hypnosis which will further illustrate what I have called the close-but-not-close-enough phenomenon.[7] It is only fair to point out that there is now much evidence available that was not then in existence.

V. M. Bechterev touched upon the reflex aspect of hypnosis.[8] "Every word, being a sign, is, in accordance with the association-reflex scheme, associated as a secondary stimulus either with an external or internal stimulus, or with some state, posture, or movement of the individual in question. The word consequently plays the role of an external stimulus, and becomes a substitute, according to the association established, for an external influence or a certain inner state."

Nevertheless, some lines further he calls hypnosis "a peculiar biological state resembling sleep." Many otherwise well-informed persons still believe this. In one of the most ingenious experiments in hypnosis it has been clearly established by Bass that ". . . sleep is not hypnosis and . . . hypnosis is neither a suggested sleep nor anything pertaining to sleep . . ."[9] At the most, sleep and hypnosis are second cousins.

Probably the most impressive of hypnotic phenomena are auditory and visual hallucinations. To watch a hypnotized subject who thinks he is talking to Napoleon, is a spectacle not easily forgotten. Even to understand the mechanism of the phenomenon does not seriously impair its drama.

The matter is clarified by an experiment of Ellson along classical Pavlovian lines.[10] His subjects sat in a comfortable Morris chair, on the left arm of which was a small light bulb. He then sounded a thousand cycle tone, which is about two octaves above middle C. The tone had a gradual onset and decline, starting, as it were, from nowhere, reaching maximum intensity several seconds after the light went on, and then fading away as it had come.

This tone, as the unconditioned stimulus, was paired for sixty trials with the "light used as a conditioned stimulus. Thirty-two of forty subjects under these conditions reported *hearing the tone when the light was presented alone.*" [Italics mine.] "Four psychologists were run through the procedure. . . . In spite of their knowledge of the purpose of the experiment, and the general procedure to be used," two of the four were conditioned into hearing auditory hallucinations. "Appropriate control groups demonstrated that the effect was not entirely due to suggestion in the instructions or test trial conditions."

It "was concluded that the conditioned sensations of the present experiment were better described as hallucinations since they were not discriminated from perceptions of a physical stimulus."

This means, less technically, that eighty per cent of the subjects in this experiment *could not tell the difference between a bona fide sound and their own hallucinations.* When we realize that sights and sounds can be conditioned, and that the bells that conjure them up may be set off internally, we can understand why Luther threw an inkwell at the devil, and from whence came the voices heard by Joan of Arc and Mohammed, to say nothing of the ghosts sincerely reported by more mundane persons.

There can be no question that hallucinations in hypnosis, and the sensory miracles associated with various saints, are essentially genuine, and explicable as phenomena of conditioning. Hunger, fatigue, and excitement, all of which reduce inhibition, would facilitate hallucinatory experiences. It may be added that in working with positive and negative visual hallucinations I have found that excellent results are usually achieved with subjects who have a fine background in art. They have established and integrated reaction systems which can be stimulated. The creation of hypnotic color blindness by Erickson is simply explicable in these terms.[11]

The discussion of hallucinations, which follows, is not meant to obtrude on anyone's religious beliefs. Religion is a matter of faith. This should be kept in mind as I discuss St. Bernadette, who has lived recently enough, and been studied enough, to provide a large body of authentic data.

Bernadette's early life was lonely. She was asthmatic, and could not attain the physical endurance of other children. She answered questions in a fashion so logical and unemotional as to seem impertinent at times. In contemporary terms we would call her emotionally inhibited.

Her hallucinations were elaborate in color and form. Later in life, as a nun, Bernadette showed great ability in drawing, and in the creation of unusual needlework. This demonstrates her elaborate series of what we may call artistic bells.

There can be no question whatever of Bernadette's complete sincerity. Her religious and artistic tendencies, and her emotionally starved childhood, provided the soil in which her hallucinations grew. Members of the Church, and learned physicians and psychiatrists, who called her visions hallucinations, were perplexed because Bernadette obviously was not insane. The more understanding of them considered Bernadette's behavior authentic. They realized that the finest actress could not simulate such a moving and deeply-seated emotional display. Hallucinations, as Ellson demonstrated, are a question of conditioning and not of sanity. In Hudgins' experiment with the pupil, and Menzies' with the ice water, we saw that the stimuli that produce conditioned responses may be originated by the subject himself. Whenever the Lady appeared, Bernadette wanted to go through her ritual exactly as it had occurred originally. To see the Lady, Bernadette clung to the same rosary, after her attempt to use another one had failed, and she wore the same clothes, having no choice at first, and refusing to change when she did. When she was asked why, the perplexed child rationalized that the clothes were part of her. Later, only after the approval of the shrine, would she wear other garments, which were always of the same type.

Everything that we know about Bernadette's hallucinations is explained quite rationally from the point of view of the conditioned reflex. Blake and Gerard[12] have even shown that mere words in regard to "light" heard by a person, can disrupt the regular beat of cells in the visual portion of the brain. By alternately talking of blindness and seeing to a subject, Loomis, Harvey, and

Hobart[13] controlled the pattern of the brain waves. They also were able to condition brain waves by turning on a light and simultaneously sounding a tone at regular intervals. Before long, the tone *alone* stopped the train of waves, although before the conditioning (and "conditioning" is in quotation marks in their original paper) the tone alone had no such effect. The human occipital alpha rhythm (one of the fundamental brain wave patterns) has been conditioned by Shagass to the voluntary act of clenching the fist.[14]

Yet Lundholm and Löwenbach found that "Hypnotically suggested light does not produce the abolition of the alpha rhythm, nor does suggested blindness prevent it."[15] I must agree with them when they say that they "are unable to explain satisfactorily the discrepancy between . . . [their] results and those of Loomis, Harvey, and Hobart." It may be that their results are functions of their techniques and the idiosyncrasies of their subjects, but I am merely guessing.

Differences in technique often mean differences in results. Kelley,[16] for example, was unable to condition auditory hallucinations, while Ellson,[17] as we saw earlier, succeeded with a different method. (Ellson, in a fine article, compares their techniques, but interestingly enough, he differentiates between hypnotic and conditioned hallucinations.[18] I do not doubt that an appropriate variation of Ellson's original technique could produce visual hallucinations, and papers by Perky[19] and Miller[20] would seem to verify this.)

With hypnosis nothing but an aspect of conditioning, we can see that it should be possible to train involuntary antisocial behavior into a subject. I find myself in agreement with Rowland,[21] Wells,[22] and Brenman [23] that appropriate procedures, which need not necessarily be subtle, can make hypnotized persons perform antisocial acts, even to the extent of criminally harming themselves or others.

As a result of hypnotic suggestion subjects have stolen money, rushed to pick up rattlesnakes, and thrown sulphuric acid into a man's face, which, unknown to the subject, was protected by invisible glass. These researches are amazing and are commended to the reader. Put bluntly, through hypnosis it is possible to force persons to commit crimes. Those who speak of the necessity for hypnotic suggestion to fit in with a subject's "moral code" should revise their concepts.

This distressing power of hypnosis is completely logical, for to the extent that one is effectively hetero-conditioned, to precisely that extent has one no effective auto-control over his own behavior. When the bell rings the appropriately trained dog salivates. He cannot help it.

My comments advocating the possibility of the hypnotic production of crimes have aroused the opposition of pollyannas who know nothing about the matter. Let me remind those who still refuse to accept what seems irrefutable, that people have been known to talk in their sleep and to utter secrets that they would rather have their tongues torn out than say volitionally. I am not saying that hypnosis is the same as sleep. I am, however, pointing out that the conception of people acting against their best interests should not startle us. We see it occasionally in sleep-walking, and in politics every day.

CHAPTER TWO

FUNDAMENTALS: HYPNOTIC REACTION PATTERNS

BEFORE further developing the relationship of hypnosis to conditioning, it will be necessary to consider an interpretation of hypnosis which has some significant adherents.

Rosenow,[1] Lundholm,[2] Pattie,[3] and Dorcus[4] have advanced an interpretation of hypnosis that seems quite impressive. It has been lucidly recapitulated and expanded by R. W. White and it is his treatment that I shall consider.[5]

White declares "hypnotic behavior is meaningful, goal-directed striving, its most general goal being to behave like a hypnotized person as this is continuously defined by the operator and understood by the subject. . . . The subject, it is held, is ruled by a wish to behave like a hypnotized person." His predominant motive is submission to the operator's commands. He "understands at all times what the operator intends, and his behavior is a striving to put these intentions into execution." It is as if the subject were playing a game, or acting a part.

I do not at all agree with this, although with slight modification I am nevertheless in complete agreement with the three specific facts that White insists must be explained by a theory of hypnotism:

That the hypnotized person can transcend the normal limits of volitional control,

That he behaves without the experience of will or intention, without the self-consciousness, and without the subsequent memory which under the circumstances one would expect, and

That these changes in his behavior occur merely because the hypnotist says so.

If we omit mention of the lack of memory, in the second point, we are left with a fine definition of a conditioned reflex:

1. There is transcendence of normal limits of volitional control. Witness Hudgins' conditioned control of the involuntary pupillary reflex.

2. The subject has no experience of will or intention. When Hudgins asked his subjects "What did you do when I said *contract?*" their answers were, "I did nothing." When a conditioned reflex is established in a subject there is no need for the subject to do anything about it. It merely happens. A subject, then, may or may not be "aware" of his conditioned reflex.

3. The changes in the subject's behavior occur merely because the hypnotist says so. This is true enough if the conditioning procedure be so conducted. When *Hudgins* conditioned pupillary contraction to his command, he (the "hypnotist") made the pupil contract. When he trained the *subject* to control his own pupil through auto-contraction, the subject could produce the results. There is no need for the concept of *rapport,* i.e., that only suggestions from the hypnotist will be accepted by the subject. The subject's reactions are dependent on what conditionings are elicited, who

elicited them, and how this was done. Considered from this point of view, the mechanism behind the autohypnotic techniques of the author becomes clear.[6] (These autohypnotic techniques form Chapter Five of this book.)

It is interesting that White does not mention Hudgins' pupillary reflex experiment, nor do the terms "conditioned reflex" or "associative reflex" appear even once in his ten thousand word discussion of the different theories of hypnosis. Nevertheless, White is to be commended that he aimed his camera in the right direction, though with blurred focus.

This close-but-not-close-enough phenomenon pervades hypnotic history. Menzies who demonstrated how a feeling of cold can be conditioned to the simultaneous presentation of light, a word, and ice water, says, in discussing the sleepiness produced in one of his subjects by the monotonous procedure, "In fact, one subject came to the conclusion that our purpose was hypnotism." The subject who believed that the purpose of the experiment was hypnotism was more accurate than the experimenter realized.

There is no evidence that the *trance* is a fundamental phenomenon of hypnosis. The trance has been variously defined, but it is generally agreed that it is a state in which deep hypnotic phenomena can be induced, particularly amnesia on awakening.

In association with William Henry Gardiner, M.D., I have trained three physically and mentally healthy adults of superior intelligence to remain completely insensitive to pain and the sounds of guns in a *waking state*. The subjects were conditioned to turn the anaesthesia on and off, *by themselves*, in any part of the body at will, in ten seconds. That the deafness to gun shots was not acting was demonstrated by the steadiness of the subjects' blood pressure whenever the gun was fired. In the usual waking state it is impossible to restrain a rise in blood pressure at a near and sudden gunshot.

Extensive experimentation has shown that there are no differences between the physiology of the hypnotic trance and the waking state. Some of the similarities in the two states are as follows:

Brain electric potentials;[7, 8, 9]
Cerebral circulation;[10]
Respiration and oxygen consumption;[11]
Respiration and heart action;[12]
Blood pressure, blood count, and blood analysis;[13]
Knee reflex.[14]

It must be realized that the experiments above are selected from others, and that they all show the identity of physiological processes in both the waking and the trance states. As for the similarities of mental activity in both states, Hull's classical book adduces dozens of experiments.[15] There can be no question. Hypnotic and waking states are not differentiated by physiological processes, thinking included.

There is no need to discuss the possible identification of hypnosis with hysteria and so-called "dissociated states." Though this belief is set forth in most neurological texts, it may fairly be regarded as disproven. White and Shevach give a fine review of the concept.[16] Yet the error of those who believe that hypnosis is a form of hysteria is true—in reverse. Hysteria is a form of conditioning. When a hysterical paralysis occurs in a person, this means that a neuro-muscular reaction has become integrated in a pattern that is considered undesirable. Hypnosis provides verbalisms of desirable integrated reaction systems. "You have regained the power of your right arm. Your fingers are strong. Your arm is strong. You can lift weights the way you did before this happened to you." Hysteria, then, is a sub-division of auto- or hetero-conditioning. It is only when the conditionings have certain so-called undesirable characteristics that they are labelled hysterical.

Davis and Husband, by using a standardized trance technique on fifty-five subjects, constructed a convenient scale for rating hypnotic susceptibility.[17] A hypnotic rating scale, based on a standardized technique, tells us what a standardized pattern of bell sounds did with a particular group of heterogeneously conditioned subjects. Hypnotic results are a function of the interaction of technique and subject. The Davis and Husband hypnotic rating scale is reproduced in full.

Score

   0 Insusceptible

   1
   2 Relaxation
   3 Fluttering of lids
   4 Closing of eyes
   5 Complete physical relaxation

   6 Catalepsy of eyes
   7 Limb catalepsies
 10 Rigid catalepsy
 11 Anaesthesia (glove)

These divisions of the scale are respectively labelled "hypnoidal" and "light trance." The rest of the scale is considered a list of medium and deep trance phenomena.

Score

   13 Partial amnesia
   15 Post-hypnotic anaesthesia
   17 Personality changes
   18 Simple post-hypnotic suggestions
   20 Kinaesthetic delusions; complete amnesia

   21 Ability to open eyes without effecting trance
   23 Bizarre post-hypnotic suggestions
   25 Complete somnambulism
   26 Positive visual hallucinations, post-hypnotic
   27 Positive auditory hallucinations, post-hypnotic
   28 Systematized post-hypnotic amnesias
   29 Negative auditory hallucinations
   30 Negative visual hallucinations; hyperaesthesias

It will be noted that all the items down to score 10 involve specific muscle activity, whether it be relaxation or catalepsy of the limb or body muscles; or fluttering, closing, or catalepsy of the eyelid muscles.

It is not a coincidence that only well-practiced muscles are affected in early hypnosis. We open and close our eyes, and move our limbs with ease. We exert constant control in the movement of the muscles involved, and it is a truism to say that the movements of our muscles are associated with the sensory information we receive from without. Consequently, words with their corresponding muscular associativity easily produce conditioned muscular responses in the much-practiced motor system of the body.

Carlson's remarkable results in treating spastic paralysis are based upon his emphasis on limiting outside sensory impressions, in order to improve muscular control.[18] He speaks "of the influence that selective inhibition of sensory stimuli has on the patient's ability to control his muscles."

There is a close parallel between his method and hypnosis conceived as conditioning. Muscle behavior is in large part a *result* of the interplay of outside sensory impressions on internal physical structures. There can be no muscular coordination without sensory and intellectual focalization. If the latter two are satisfactory, the muscles will take care of themselves.[19] It will be of interest here to note that Livingood reports the successful use of hypnosis with a case of spastic paralysis.[20] He has since successfully used the autohypnotic techniques of the author in the same case.[21]

The fundamental concept of "mental alienation" in the Kenny treatment of infantile paralysis has a somewhat similar common denominator, although Kenny has emphatically denied any similarity of her method with hypnosis. What, after all, is involved in much of her magnificent method but conditioning an awareness of muscular control?

Her formula for the destruction of "mental alienation"—and the production of mental control—might be simplified as follows:

Technician touches a specific muscle pattern of child.
Technician tells child to think of the muscle involved.
Child, by association, gains ideo-motor control of the muscles involved.

The parallelism to the explanation of hypnosis I have been presenting is striking. There are elaborate techniques available for the reconditioning of the physically handicapped, and reconditioning is even possible following actual structural damage to the cortex.

All of us have seen, with some surprise, bruises on our body that indicated severe injuries, yet there was no pain at their onset, because our attention was then engaged elsewhere. Consequently, verbalisms about a lack of sensitivity and an absence of feeling can release *established* reaction systems of anaesthesia. As for amnesia, we have all had at least slight lapses of memory. Consequently, verbalisms in regard to forgetting find trained neural patterns ready to receive them and to be elicited.

The complicated phenomena of post-hypnotic suggestion are nothing but a series of conditioned speech and muscle acts. In the creation of moods in a subject, glandular conditionings may be involved, and previously established feelings are sympathetically vibrated: "You are bored," or "you are happy, very happy." Unskilled hypnotists often condition a muscular inhibition: "You will not bite your nails." "You will not tremble in front of an audience."

Krasnogorski, a disciple of Pavlov, has demonstrated that in children the ease of reflex formation increases with intelligence.[22] It is impossible to establish conditioned reflexes in congenital idiots, but in the higher types of mental defectives reflexes can be conditioned, though only with difficulty and for short duration. In normally intelligent children the reflexes are easily conditioned.

If intelligence is associated with ease of conditioning, we would also expect intelligence to be associated with ease of hypnotizability. And in fact, there is extensive evidence that this is the case.

Clinicians working in the older tradition have always known that hypnotizability goes with intelligence. Lloyd has said that the better the intelligence, generally speaking, the better the subject, if he can be hypnotized at all.[23] Tuckey also emphasizes this and speaks of "the fallacy of the contention which one sometimes hears urged against hypnotism, that it is only applicable to fools and weaklings."[24] It is easy to hypnotize intelligent children, and almost impossible to hypnotize dull ones.

These observations have been verified in the laboratory. White found that the students with higher college marks were somewhat better hypnotic subjects than those with lower ones.[25] He found that high scores in a college level intelligence test had a positive relationship with hypnotizability, and Davis and Husband, using the American Council of Education scholastic aptitude tests, found a similar and stronger correlation.[26] Hull presents a page of similar positive correlations.[27]

Hull, who said, "words . . . are assumed . . . to have acquired during the previous history of the subject, through the process of association or conditioning, the capacity to evoke the reactions of which they are the names," calls the conditioned reflex "one of the most primitive of all learning and memory processes."[28] In a broad sense, then, there should be no occasion for surprise that intelligence helps, rather than hinders, the acquisition of hypnosis. I cannot forbear quoting Hull further:

Practice in the act [of hypnosis] facilitates its performance; the rate of gain is more rapid early in the practice than later; a period of disuse is followed by a partial loss of the facilitation resulting from practice; the amount of loss from disuse is greater where the practice intervals are closely spaced; a resumption of practice produces a recovery of the lost facility; the curve of the recovery is one of negative acceleration; and the general rate of recovery of facility is faster than was its original acquisition at the point in question.

Such a remarkable and detailed conformity of the phenomena of hypnosis to the known experimental characteristics of ordinary habituation can hardly be accidental and without significance. The indication would seem to be that, whatever else hypnosis may be, it is—to a considerable extent, at least—a habit phenomenon and that quite possibly this hypothesis may furnish the basis for an ultimate understanding and explanation of its hitherto largely inexplicable characteristics.

This is indeed so. Hypnosis is an accident in the development of history. It is an aspect of conditioning. In science, the specific phenomenon usually precedes the general theory. Conditioning is an instrument of the most fantastic power, and the person under treatment needs neither faith, nor hope, nor confidence, for satisfactory psychotherapy.

After all this overwhelming laboratory evidence that hypnosis is an aspect of conditioning, we can see how far-fetched and impertinent is the Freudian belief that in hypnotism the *hypnotist plays the role of the subject's parent of the opposite sex.* Actually, the psychoanalytic explanation of hypnosis need not be taken seri ously. Freud himself wrote, ". . . the mechanism of hypnosis is so enigmatical to me that I would not like to refer to it as an explanation."[29] And thirty years later he wrote, "Now that I once more approach the riddle of suggestion after having kept away from it for some thirty years, I find there is no change in the situation. . . . there has been no explanation of the nature of suggestion . . ."[30]

The psychoanalytic conception of hypnosis is probably the greatest exaggeration in the entire history of psychiatry, for it is from the seed of this completely unfounded and discredited misconception that the *entire* psychoanalytic structure has grown. Freud himself bore witness to this crucial relationship between hypnotism and psychoanalysis. "The importance of hypnotism for the history of the development of psychoanalysis must not be too lightly estimated. Both in *theoretic as well as in therapeutic aspects,** psychoanalysis is the administrator of the estate left by hypnotism."[31] And baldly put, Freud and his disciples never had the remotest notion of what hypnosis is all about. Starting with false premises they could only arrive at false conclusions.

Surely, to say that hypnosis is an aspect of conditioning, and that it is a historical accident in our way of talking about behavior, makes matters look suspiciously simple. But as Morris R. Cohen said, "If *per impossible* any theory were as complicated as the actual facts, it would have no real value. All theory is a simplification and therefore incomplete."[32] As long as special assump-

---

* Italics mine.

tions and qualifications are not introduced, thus making the simplicity deceptive, the simplicity may be considered valid.[33]

Once when I expressed my views on hypnosis, it was objected that I weakened my position by "a tendency to employ chiefly those references that support" my views.[34] Even if this were so, it is a specious objection, for the pertinent issue is whether references are true in fact, and logically implicative, and such is indeed the case.

Curiously, precisely the opposite accusation has been made elsewhere, alleging that my position "is not supported by adequate data."[35] In essence, both criticisms are ways of rejecting what is contrary to personal preference.

Those who hold that I have confused the altered hypnotic state of the individual with the method of induction, are unwittingly accepting my point of view. It is poor reasoning to admit that the hypnotic procedure involves a subject's conditioned reflexes, and to deny that the subject's hypnotic "state" involves those same reflexes, chronologically advanced.

Methodologically unsound are those who say, for example, "This results in some new formulations, but no new insight into the psychodynamic principles of hypnosis."[36] Or, "Throughout . . . one senses the lack of any frame of reference for the understanding of human personality."[37]

The conditioned reflex, as anyone who has studied elementary psychology will know, is a frame of reference for the understanding of human personality, and auxiliary thereto, for understanding the "psychodynamic principles of hypnosis." Persons are privileged to differ with my frame of reference, but they are not well grounded if they do not recognize one when they encounter it.

Milton H. Erickson has published some violent strictures which could be overlooked had they not appeared in a reputable psychiatric journal.[38] Aside from arguing *ad hominem* he makes that classically deceptive scholarly statement, "Authors are discussed out of context . . . armchair statements are made." If the reader will check my sources, he will find these criticisms to be completely without foundation. Scientific criticism at such a level is not only unfair to the person whose work is being considered, but also tends to lower the intellectual integrity of the publication in which it appears.

A fairly complete recapitulation of the objections to my ideas is that of Brenman and Gill.[39] I quote it in its entirety, and have numbered the paragraphs for convenience. The brackets and italics are mine.

1. The last type of theory which we will mention is that of hypnosis as a conditioned reflex. This theory has lately been revived by Salter. It was the basis of Hilger's theory [the authors might have credited Pavlov and Bechterev] in the first decade of this century. In essence it states that since an individual forms associations between words and sensations, the word as a conditioned stimulus can call forth the reaction which is evoked by the situation which the word describes. It seems to us that this is a *superficial* statement of the problem which fails to take into account the specificity of the hypnotic state, the possible physiological basis of hypnosis as a conditioned reflex, or the motivational factors involved in hypnosis.

2. *It may be that conditioned reflexes do play some role*

in some of the phenomena elicitable in the hypnotic state. Kubie has also suggested that "the subject who has been hypnotized many times inevitably develops certain automatic or conditioned reflexes by which a short-cut is established to the hypnotic state."

3. To discuss the conditioned reflex theory of hypnosis adequately would raise the whole problem of explaining complex human behavior as conditioned reflex, a problem which we do not feel it advisable to discuss here.

It will be noticed that this passage progressively nullifies itself. Paragraph one says that to consider hypnosis a conditioned reflex is "superficial," the simplicity objection in another guise. In paragraph two, the authors, being persons of integrity, meditated for a while and then added, *"It may be that conditioned reflexes do play some role."* After thinking a bit longer, in paragraph three they conclude that "to discuss the conditioned reflex theory of hypnosis adequately would raise the whole problem of explaining complex human behavior as conditioned reflex, a problem which we do not feel it advisable to discuss here."

And that is the crux of the question. A theory of hypnosis can lead only to a theory of human behavior, and vice versa. I have explained my theory of human behavior elsewhere.[40] At this point suffice it to say that the conditioned reflex theory of hypnosis is validly inferred, and emerges unscathed from the objections raised against it.

CHAPTER THREE

PRELIMINARY EXPERIMENTS
IN AUTOHYPNOSIS

AS WE have seen, "hypnosis" and "trance" are terms of convenience which have become attached to aspects of conditioning. It is from this point of view that the following problem suggested in an earlier paper of the author will be considered.[1] "To what extent can auto-hypnotic subjects be trained to get their results in a waking state by their own post-hypnotic suggestion, and thus obviate the necessity for their own trances?" In short, how can subjects be taught complete hypnotic control of themselves in a *waking* state.

There were fifty-six subjects in this experiment. They ranged in age from nineteen to thirty-two, and one was forty-eight. Thirty-five of the subjects were men and twenty-one were women. They were obtained from employment agencies and by asking them to bring friends.

The subjects will be numbered in the order of their interviews. Thus, M-43 means that the subject was male and was the forty-third subject interviewed, and F-13 means that the subject was female and was the thirteenth subject. The order of interview is relevant and will be commented upon. Only the subjects of interest will be discussed and the purpose, technique, and results varied from one subject to another.

They were tested separately, or from two to five at a time. They were told the conditioning concepts of hypnosis, and that only those chosen would be paid. Many of the subjects found the experiments so interesting and helpful that they refused money for their services. Although all of them knew in advance that hypnosis was the problem being investigated, and had been warned with deliberate inaccuracy that only one in ten would be satisfactory, it was the impression that many of them came out of curiosity.

After a half-hour lecture, all of their questions were answered. They were then given four minutes of verbalisms of heaviness, tiredness, and lid closure. Some subjects could not open their eyes, and suggestions were then given of ability to do so.

The subjects were next interviewed singly, and those whose reports showed promise were asked to return for a second and individual test. It was considered promising for a subject to report that he felt "very comfortable"—or, "I feel so relaxed now," or "I could just go to sleep," or, of course, could not open his eyes although some of the best subjects did not come from this latter group.

At the second session the subject was given individual sleeping hypnosis for approximately ten minutes, and then awakened and asked to report his feelings. As the experiment went along, what I may call the "feed-back" method was developed, and it was found to produce good subjects with great ease.

Basically speaking, the "feed-back" method involves giving the subject a series of short verbal conditionings, after which he is asked to report his feelings. Some will say, "I felt as if the world went far away." Others will report the dominance of relaxed feelings. Some will confess to a "loss of control over myself." When verbal conditionings are next administered to the subject, their motif is whatever predominant quality the subject had previously reported. In other words, rather than persistently ringing standard verbal bells as is usually done, the subject's individual conditionings are found and fed back to him. This method was developed more sharply as the experiment continued, and is the reason for the excellent subjects' having high interview numbers.

Three groups of subjects will be considered, and in the reverse order of their interest.

Group   I. Those of miscellaneous interest.
Group   II. Check of feed-back method.
Group III. Intensive study of feed-back method.

Discussion of Group I

M-4 was a twenty-year-old college student. He seemed politely introverted. The usual hypnotic procedure had been used with him, and each time produced what may best be described as a state of isolation, in which he was not especially amenable to suggestion.

On his fourth test period, he was thoroughly questioned, and it was found that at the age of fifteen he had developed the habit of putting himself into a trance-like state whenever he wished to evade reality and get a rest. He had done so at least one hundred times since then, "probably more." Experimentation was discontinued after eliciting this information. All that the hypnotic procedure had done in this instance was to hit the various conditioned bells he had already established in himself.

F-13 was twenty-six years of age, of superior intelligence and extremely quiet. On her first individual test, full anaesthesias were elicited and a thorough amnesia reported. The anaesthesia was demonstrated post-hypnotically, and its intensity perplexed her, for she had not believed that she would be a good subject. On her third session she awakened spontaneously, and confessed under pressure that she did not like this at all, and had decided to fight between "obedience and non-obedience" during the administration of the trance verbalisms. Her services were discontinued immediately. Here was a conflict between internal and external processes. I am of the opinion that if the external hypnotic verbalizations had been differently constructed this subject could nevertheless have been conditioned against her will.

The only features of interest with subjects F-14 and M-19 were the intensive personality changes elicited, especially in the former.

F-29 reported that the trance procedure made her feel "less worried." Conversation revealed that she had been suffering from a hysterical lump in the throat for the past five years as a sequel of a painful marriage. This is an extraordinary case, and it is my intention to report it in full detail on another occasion.

Under hypnosis, the subject with copious tears relived her painful experiences. On awakening, with a conditioned total amnesia, she reported a feeling of great relief. On being hypnotized again and told she would remember everything upon awakening, she reported that she felt "as if a great weight had been lifted from my shoulders." She has discontinued the use of sleeping pills and powders, and the globus hystericus is gone.

This subject was the first one with whom there began the concept of the feed-back technique.

F-35 had a complete amnesia and anaesthesia, and the various classical phenomena were elicited. She was an excellent subject for experimentation and was taught to give herself suggestions of confidence before applying for a position. She thereby secured excellent employment, which she had not expected, and she was therefore no longer available for experimentation. She refused payment for her services. The feed-back method was further modified with this subject .

M-43 was quickly developed into an excellent subject, and reported that it made him feel as if he were receiving laughing gas from a dentist. The dental situation was thoroughly verbalized by him, as a means of assisting the experimenter to discover and compound appropriate verbal conditionings. Laughter and jubilation were easily induced, and the anaesthesia was conditioned to become progressively intensive.

He complained jokingly, but accurately, that he had

become extravagant after each session of "hypnotic laughing gas," and that he had found his interests in reading to be changing back to his happier post-adolescent days. Here was a person with an unhappy maturity, who, on feeling exhilarated for the first time "in many years," recaptured the mood and activities of a happier era. The effect of mood on behavior was thoroughly studied with him. Hypnotically produced moods can provide intensive drives to help a subject carry out his program of psychotherapeutic re-education.

Discussion of Group II

Group II was composed of F-48, F-49, and M-54. These subjects were used to verify the feed-back method.

F-48, after her second session, was told that upon awakening she would write down how it felt to be "in a trance," and would then go back to sleep. She did so with a hazy recollection of the trance. Her report declared that she felt "without will of my own, and under your power." The additional verbal conditioning which she received was developed along these lines, and intensive anaesthesias were elicited. A gun was fired after appropriate suggestions of deafness were given. There was no perceptible reaction.

As her dominant sensation, F-49 reported "relaxation and ease," and she was developed accordingly. In this instance it was decided to experiment with the production of personality changes. It is my impression that through these methods excellent acting can become a simple accomplishment.

M-54 was the last member of this group. Discussion with him developed the fact that the sound level of the outside world had seemed to subside. Satisfactory cutaneous and auditory anaesthesias were elicited. Difficulty in his availability for appointment made it necessary to discontinue experimentation with him.

CHAPTER FOUR

A STUDY OF GROUP III

G ROUP III will be the last considered; specifically, subjects M-40, F-47, and M-52. They will be studied in careful detail, and will illustrate the relevancy of the insights gained from my other subjects. I would like once more to express my gratitude for the excellent coöperation extended to me by William Henry Gardiner, M.D., in the physical studies of these subjects.

M-40 was a bright and healthy young man of twenty-one. He later joined the Naval Air Force, and his physical, mental, and emotional ratings upon acceptance were the highest ever scored in the service.

Suggestions of auditory anaesthesia were not at first successful, but in the second individual session he reported a substantial deafness. This was brought about in the feed-back by comparing hearing to a radio. "While you are wide-awake and I count from ten back to one, your hearing will fade gradually, as if the world were coming through a radio and the volume were being reduced from normal intensity to zero, except for the sound of my voice. That will remain the same. In order to bring the sound back, I merely have to count from one to ten, and your hearing will return gradually. At ten it will all be back."

This suggestion was followed out successfully, except

that on counting backwards to one, the final intensity was not a complete absence of sound. He had been given an amnesia for these conditionings, and when it was suggested to him in the waking state that the radio analogy for shutting off the sound was a good one, he agreed that it well described what had occurred to him.

He was again hypnotized and told the same, except that the radio analogy was expounded in greater detail and more vigorously. This time it was completely successful, as measured by his inability to localize the position of the experimenter in the room as the latter walked around in back of him. The floor was pounded to see if the subject reported any vibration. He did. When hands were clapped near his ears, he reported no hearing, but a feeling as if he had suddenly dived under water. He was again hypnotized, and pressure and vibration feelings were removed.

At the next session the subject was conditioned to give himself appropriate mental verbalizations for the production of deafness to all sounds but the experimenter's voice. A loud 22-caliber starter's gun was fired off twice, about four feet in back of him. He in no way flinched or moved. This was later verified with moving pictures. Ten hours of experimentation were devoted to this subject. The gun was fired frequently, and blood pressure recordings were taken simultaneously.

A typical session follows:

The subject induced an auditory anaesthesia, and his blood pressure was found to be 122. The gun was fired and he in no way reacted. The subject then brought back his hearing. He was then told that the gun would soon be fired. His pressure jumped to 138. (All subjects had an increase in their normal blood pressure when they were told that the gun was going to be fired.) About ten seconds later the gun was fired, and his pressure rose to 154. His blood pressure was allowed to subside, and it remained steady at 128. He was not told that the gun would be fired again. At the sudden gunshot his pressure jumped from 128 to 140. In some sessions the non-prepared shot without auditory anaesthesia preceded the announced auditory anaesthesia, but there was no significant difference in results.

It was soon noticed that the subject received sensory cues. He had been deliberately told, after a while, that some situations involved gunshots—for example, when the experimenter discussed current events and walked about the room, or read fables whose meaning he was asked to give. As these situations were repeated, he reported "a feeling that the gun was going to go off," and he would brace himself for it.

At intervals a phonograph recording of an air raid was played at varying sound levels at the back of the room. The firing of anti-aircraft guns, the roar of motors, and the dropping of bombs were intense. Problems in simple arithemetic were given to the subject in a low voice, and questions were asked such as:[1]

> How is a bird different from a dog?
> What are tables made of?
> What is cotton good for?
> What are gloves made of?
> What are envelopes made of?
> In what ways are a knife, a chisel, and a saw alike?

The experimenter had an elaborate series of signals to Dr. Gardiner, who operated the air-raid recording.

These signals involved the manipulation of a cigarette lighter or a pencil, and at no time did the subject apprehend their meaning.

The experimenter endeavored to keep his voice at a low standard pitch and intensity, and most of the time he could not hear his own voice above the din. The subject sat calmly and with eyes shut. The answers of the subject were judged by his lip movements.

It was found that there was a certain level of sound above which the subject reported that he heard nothing, or only a vague vibration. Apparently the brain can filter sounds to a certain extent, but there was a point beyond which the voice of the experimenter and the sound of the air-raid blended in an unrecognizable distortion pattern of sound waves.

On several occasions, when the subject was not self-deafened, the bombardment record was suddenly turned on without warning at a loud intensity. The subject immediately jerked his head in alarm to find the source of the disturbance. When, in this undeafened state he was told to listen to the shooting of the revolver and the different intensities at which the air-raid record had been played, he at first refused to believe that he had not heard them. He emphatically declared that I had told him that these sounds had been administered to him and that he had not heard them, only in order to study his reactions. He knew very well that it was impossible not to hear such sounds. He was finally convinced and said, reluctantly, "If you say so, I suppose you're telling the truth."

There were several control tests of the ability to distinguish language during auditory interruptions, without autohypnotic deafness. In general, there seemed to be a better filtering of interruptions in the state of auditory anaesthesia.

Another series of control experiments was performed with differing pairs of un-anaesthetized subjects, equidistant from the experimenter, and at varying distances from the source of the sound. The auditorily anaesthetized subject could differentiate material with much greater ease than the untrained subjects. The auditory capacities of the latter, however, were tested only approximately. This aspect of the experiment should be repeated. These control experiments were performed with similar results with the other members of Group III.

This subject was also conditioned to produce an anaesthesia at will in any part of his body, while remaining in the so-called waking state. In order to produce this anaesthesia, the subject had merely to concentrate on the part of his body in which he wished the absence of feeling, and to think "The feeling is going away. The feeling is going away. The feeling is going away." This was conditioned to produce a complete anaesthesia. In order to restore sensation, the subject had to think "The feeling is coming back. The feeling is coming back. The feeling is coming back." That would suffice. All subjects were similarly trained to anaesthetize themselves.

The subject would inflict perceptible injuries upon himself with a sterilized needle and knife point as he explored his anaesthesias. After a while he was not allowed to check them because it was found that this subject, as well as the other two members of this group, inflicted deep injuries upon himself in his surprise at the utter absence of feeling. All the subjects laughed and denied that they enjoyed any masochistic pleasure in their self-punishment. "It isn'ᵗ punishment," they said.

As measured by verbal reports, and the absence of flinching and changes in blood pressure, the anaesthesia was complete and thorough. All those who were good subjects were surprised at being so. Nobody believed "it could happen to me."

This subject at first disliked the bodily and auditory anaesthesia. "It's kind of frightening that things like this can go on about you without your knowing it." He would check his hearing by snapping his fingers near his ears, clapping his hands, or knocking on the chair or desk. He would verify his skin anaesthesias by pinching and prodding himself. On most occasions, when he found that he had produced the anaesthesias, he would shake his head incredulously.

As was said earlier, the conditioned reflex explanation of hypnosis had been given to him before the experimentation had begun. Although he admitted that it sounded logical, and probably explained the phenomena, he found it difficult not to be amazed at them.

It is the general opinion in the literature that an attitude of prestige and polite distance with hypnotic subjects is of primary importance for successful results. I do not agree with this. In these experiments, although the reputation of the experimenter was known to the subjects, everything was discussed and done with great and deliberate informality. I believe that sustaining an attitude of prestige and distance toward a subject is essentially unimportant. All that is involved is conditioning.

F-47 was a distinctly intelligent and attractive young woman of twenty-two. Her education had been limited to high school, from which she was graduated at fifteen. She gave an impression of alertness and mental stability, and this latter was verified by a Bernreuter Personality Inventory which was given to her after her seventh session.

It was found that she was less neurotic than 95 per cent of the adult female population. She was slightly above average in self-sufficiency (57.2 per cent) and more extroverted than 90 per cent of women. She was more dominant than 95.2 per cent of women and her high dominance score, which her behavior verified, had no effect on her hypnotizability. She was distinctly self-confident and sociable—more so than 92 per cent of women. Here, then, was a well-adjusted personality.

On awakening from her first individual trance, one in which she had received conditionings of deafness to all sound but my voice, she looked around quizzically and asked, "Is this room sound-proofed? It's very quiet here."

In order to gather more information for the feed-back, I asked her to explain further. "Well," she said, "it's like a radio studio. It's quiet and sound-proof. When you don't say anything you can almost hear the silence. Does this make any sense to you?"

I told her that I thought I understood.

She had a complete amnesia, and when I dropped my pencil to the desk from a distance of about a foot she looked puzzled and said, "What's this?" She had not heard the pencil drop, for she had been told that she would hear nothing but the experimenter's voice.

The experimenter clapped his hands slowly, and asked her what he had done. She said that he had merely brought his hands together. He smiled deliberately. The subject then knocked on the wooden arms of her chair. She knocked again and again, more vigorously. She knocked on the experimenter's desk. She snapped her fingers near her ears, and heard nothing.

"Hello, hello," she said aloud, and seemed relieved to hear her voice. "Say something," she asked the experimenter.

"Isn't this interesting?" I said.

"It is," she replied, "and I don't like it at all."

To facilitate training, this subject, as well as all the others, had been conditioned to fall asleep instantly when the experimenter snapped his fingers and said "fast asleep." This was done, and she fell asleep instantly.

She was then told that the silence would be deeper than ever. "Just like a radio studio. Thoroughly sound-proofed and so pleasant. So very quiet. As if the walls were absorbing every sound—every single sound, but the sound of my voice." This was expounded further. The subject was then told that the silence would always be very "soothing and relaxing. So comfortable. So pleasant."

She was then awakened, and after about a half minute spontaneously remarked how quiet and pleasant everything was. It was not the way it had been before.

This was "wonderful." The conditioning had been effective.

When my co-worker in the experiment, Dr. Gardiner, walked up to her without her hearing him, she became quite alarmed. "I don't like this at all," she said. She paused for a while. "I don't suppose it's so bad after all. You get used to this thing as you go along." Note the rationalization. In reality, neither her feelings nor her statements were her own, but she did not realize this.

At the next session she was taught to produce an anaesthesia, in a waking state, in any part of the body. Since the anaesthesia had first been produced while a conditioned paralysis of her right arm remained, every auto-induced anaesthesia thereafter brought a spontaneous paralysis of the part of the body involved.

When she was given a sterilized burr-headed needle, and told to explore her self-anaesthetized right arm, in an effort to verify this she produced a series of skin punctures, some of which bled. When she brought back the feeling, the traumatized portions were painful, and she complained strenuously. She was told to remove the feeling from the injuries until they healed. With a few seconds of thought she did so, and then she no longer gave any attention to her arms. All subjects could produce this self-limiting anaesthesia for injuries. This particular subject used it successfully with a case of painful menstruation from which she had suffered since adolescence.

She was then reconditioned to auto-controlled deafness to all sounds except voices. The deafness was modified in this way for all subjects in Group III because it had been found that when only the experi-

menter's voice could be heard, the subjects were often
distressed. In practical military operations, of course,
such a modification would be essential.

The usual gunshots and air-raid recordings were used
as stimuli. Her auto-conditioned auditory anaesthesia
was verified on many occasions by the absence of all
noticeable responses and by blood pressure checks.
Once, when the gun was fired as a check shot without
warning, and without auditory anaesthesia, the subject
became alarmed, wept, and was violently disturbed.
Some psychologically untutored spectators were convinced this behavior was fraudulent and in poor taste.
When this was told to the subject she objected vigorously. It may be added that the uninformed spectators
changed their minds after they themselves had checked
her auto-induced cutaneous anaesthesias.

This subject was demonstrated to Dr. Margaret
Brenman, who cross-examined her thoroughly with regard to her attitude toward the experimenter. However,
nothing was elicited that indicated resentment, or
equated him to a father substitute as called for by the
psychoanalytic belief that the hypnotist plays the role
of the subject's parent of the opposite sex. This belief
is not entirely without foundation, however, for in
selected cases it is conceivable that such have been the
personal conditionings of the subject.

At Dr. Brenman's request the subject anaesthetized
her left hand. On it Dr. Brenman then traced simple
geometric designs again and again with her finger. The
subject, whose eyes were closed, was asked to report the
shape of the tracings. She thought for a while and said
that she did not "have the faintest idea."

When she was pressed to exert great effort and make the best guess that she could, she said, "Circle." The tracing was actually a triangle.

This test was an effort to check the dissociation approach, for if anaesthesia is so explained, it is possible that the bonds might not always be completely severed and the subject's "guess" could be correct. These were the only tests performed by Dr. Brenman. Although it was quite interesting to watch her excellent technique with the subject, the question is not one of dissociation, but one of conditioning.

On another occasion the same subject autohypnotically induced anesthesias of the face, head, and eyes. The latter were explored with a sterilized finger tip. The eye test does not mean much, because many individuals can permit the cornea to be touched without any overt reaction. This subject could also do so, but stimulation of an anaesthetized eye produced considerably less flinching.

In total anesthesias of the head, the subject reported a feeling as if she were compressed in a shell. She pinched her cheeks, and explored her face, and declared that this was very uncomfortable mentally. It will be noted that the phenomena were produced despite the subject's complaints. She could easily have been conditioned to "like" the procedures, but this was not felt to be fair. In this connection I must again repeat my belief that appropriate hypnotic technique can unquestionably produce a liking for anti-social behavior in subjects, their so-called moral code notwithstanding.

Here is an especially interesting series of tests. The subject induced anaesthesia of the entire right arm.

This was then explored with a painful burr-shaped needle, and the overt reactions and conversation of the subject, and the blood pressure studies, left no doubt as to the completeness of the anaesthesia.

Although the anaesthesia was still present, the subject was next told to induce a glove anaesthesia of the right hand. She protested that she could not make it any more anaesthetic than it was. "I just don't realize that my arm exists below the shoulder." She was told, nevertheless, to induce a glove anaesthesia. She did so, and protested that it was "silly," and that "you can't feel less than nothing."

The right arm was explored, and it was as anaesthetic as ever. The subject was then told to induce another anaesthesia of the entire arm. She watched as this anaesthesia was checked and said, "See. You didn't have to have me do this again."

The subject was then told to remove the anaesthesia of the arm. She went through the ritual of thinking, "The feeling is coming back. The feeling is coming back. The feeling is coming back." The arm was again explored, and to the subject's alarm, the anaesthesia was still complete, the first time she had ever found this to occur.

"I don't like this at all," she said, and became agitated. An effort was made to calm her, and she was instructed to remove the anaesthesia from her entire right arm again. She did so, and the arm was again explored. The anesthesia seemed to have vanished, but she said that from the wrist down she felt the needle slightly, but not as painfully as it usually felt when feeling was unimpaired.

She was then instructed to give mental verbalizations to her hand that the feeling was returning there. Upon exploration she reported that it appeared that her hand was "all right now." In order to calm her further, she was then instructed to tell herself that the feeling had returned to her entire arm. She did so.

The subject then remarked, "I don't like this at all. Why didn't it work before?"

A theory was quickly compounded for her, that is, that the conditionings for anaesthesia had, as it were, locked the door several times, and to open the door effectively it had to be unlocked as many times as it had been locked. Although created at the spur of the moment, this is probably a felicitous analogy, although in terms of the mechanisms involved it remains difficult to explain, and I shall not venture a guess.

It was not verified whether this was a function of the subject, or of the phenomena involved. That the subject may have thought that the door had to be unlocked as many times at is had been locked is a possibility, but nothing in the procedure was calculated to give her such an impression, and her behavior also belied such an interpretation.

This may be a relevant parallel. In the production of auditory anaesthesias, subjects often produced deafness upon themselves several times consecutively, i.e., they locked the door again and again. Nevertheless, they were able to unlock it on their first effort—although they often pressed their ears as if they had just left the water after swimming. They would snap their fingers near their ears, and would rap on the chair and desk and say, "Yes, it's all right now."

It may be asked whether these additional verbalisms served to unlock the door a number of times at least equal to the number of times it had been locked. Here indeed is an interesting problem.

A study of subject M-52 will bring this chapter to a close. This young man was twenty years old and had attended college for two years. He gave the same straight-forward impression as the two previously discussed subjects.

He was given a Bernreuter Personality Inventory at the end of the seventh session and he was found to be distinctly normal and well integrated. Specifically, he was more stable emotionally than 76 per cent of the male population, average in his self-sufficiency (50.2 per cent) and more extroverted than 64 per cent of males. He was more dominant and confident than 75 per cent of the male population, and distinctly sociable —more so than 80 per cent of the population. Hypnotizability as a function of submissiveness or neuroticism is definitely contra-indicated by these experiments.

This subject had been filtered from a group after he had given adequate responses to several minutes of hypnotic suggestion. By the end of the third individual session, he had been trained to auto-induce auditory and deep cutaneous anaesthesias, and to remain in a waking state while doing this. At first he reported feelings of pressure, without sound, when the gun was fired near him. He, as well as the other two subjects, compared the feeling in the ears to the experience of diving under water. Through the feed-back method he was taught to reduce the "depth" of the water, and he soon reported an absence of pressure feelings.

The subjects in Group III did not suffer from any ringing or pain in their ears when they were experimented upon while under auditory anaesthesia. This had been conditioned away. There was also no decrease in their general efficiency between sessions. If anything, their efficiency and feelings of well-being were improved. F-47, previously discussed, reported headaches at the start of experimentation, but they stopped when her attitude was corrected. These headaches had existed with both cutaneous and auditory anaesthesias.

The male subject now being considered had reported that the feeling of silence was like that which he had once experienced when he visited the Carlsbad Caverns in New Mexico. Visitors there are brought to an extremely quiet corner of the caverns, and all the lights are put out. The feeling of silence and isolation is overwhelming. This information was used in the feed-back.

This subject, as well as the other two, reported that when he successfully induced auditory anaesthesias, to all sounds except voices, his own sounded hollow to him. "It's as if my head is empty—and my voice is making an echo inside." This was conditioned to be comfortable.

All subjects expressed surprise when the phenomena were induced. On one occasion, when his conditioning was in the hetero-controlled stage, this subject was told that when the experimenter counted from ten backwards to one, all sounds except voices would disappear. This was effective, and all sounds were then brought back.

The subject then said that he did not believe it would

work when the experimenter was not in the same room with him. He was sent into the adjoining room, where, through the open door, he could hear the experimenter's voice counting backwards from ten to one. Through the window, the subject watched a woman walking down the street with a clatter of heels. He was astonished to find that as the woman approached his window, and the experimenter continued counting, the sound of her footsteps had decreased in intensity to zero.

At first all of the subjects toyed with the production of auditory anaesthesias while visiting friends or walking on the street. They stopped this when they found that it was always effective. The experimenter had warned them that they might be injured by automobiles which they did not hear. It must be emphasized that the problem of the deleterious effect of autohypnosis exists more in theory than in actuality, and even if it did exist it could be conditioned away.

This subject was able to comprehend conversation during the playing of the recorded air-raid, but the importance of sensory cues was again illustrated, for when he realized what was about to be done, he would sometimes flinch at a gunshot. If it were totally unexpected, and occurred in a situational context that *he had not known* was associated with an actual gunshot, he at no time reported any awareness of it. This was objectively verified.

For a while he was taught to *drop* his blood pressure when the gun went off. That would mean that he became more relaxed when the revolver went off five feet from his ear, and the sound reverberated from the walls. He said he did not hear the gun, yet obviously it had registered within him, for his blood pressure would drop instantly.

Most of the experiments with this subject were devoted to cutaneous anaesthesias. In conditioning the anaesthesias, realization of limb position had also been removed. Full anaesthesia to pressure and pain, and to warmth and cold, was conditioned into all of the subjects, so that a subject could in no way feel the anaesthetized portion being stimulated.

On one occasion between sessions, the subject spilled some hot coffee on his lap, and received an extremely painful burn. He reminded himself of his anaesthetic capacity, and anaesthetized the areas involved. It was still badly scarred several months later. It should be noticed here that the subject had no difficulty in turning on the anaesthesia *after* the onset of trauma. The military significance of this should be patent. There is no need for the subject to anaesthetize himself before being wounded, and he can shut off the anaesthesia whenever it is diagnostically necessary.

Foster Kennedy, M.D., expressed interest in the anaesthetic portion of the experiment, and performed two ingenious tests with this subject. He first told him to anaesthetize the lower third of the inside of the right arm, somewhat above the wrist. Dr. Kennedy did not touch the area, but merely pointed to it. He then carefully explored the arm to delimit the area. He found that the anaesthetized area was not precisely the one to which he had referred.

The subject agreed, with the comment that he had found it difficult to think of the area to be anaesthetized. He said that if he had been permitted to touch it, he would have succeeded completely, although he had nevertheless successfully chosen about 90 per cent of it. The borders of the area, extending to the sides of the arm, did not coincide with the desired periphery.

In the second test the experimenter placed the palm side of his hand on the subject's bare back, below the right shoulder blade. He kept contact for approximately two seconds, and then told the subject to anaesthetize the area. Exploration showed results similar to those reported above. Most of the area was appropriately anaesthetized, in this case an inner 80 per cent.

These tests clearly show that the subject produces the lack of feeling where he *believes* he is supposed to produce it, and only to the extent to which he can mentally localize the area. This capacity for mental localization varies in different parts of the body. The outlines of the anaesthetized portions in no way resembled those found in anaesthesias caused by organic lesions.

In the last series of tests with this subject he produced anaesthesias of both arms, which were thoroughly checked, and found to be complete and permeating. The subject nevertheless was able to write, operate a typewriter, and lift objects as if he had no anaesthesia at all. Strength and control were unimpaired. He said that it made him uncomfortable not to feel the pencil and typewriter keys, nor the contact sensation as he lifted a chair. He had a vague feeling of strain in other parts of his body. "When I lift something it's as if I'm lifting it, and not lifting it at the same time." He explained that he did not feel any strain in his hands or arms, but felt some tension in his back.

At this juncture, J. P. McEvoy, the author, who is a

jiujitsu expert, proceeded to put the subject through a series of jiujitsu grips used to reduce a person to instant submission. The cracking of the joints of the subject was distinctly audible, but he reported no feeling of pain at all and did not flinch, writhe, or jump in any fashion. His face remained relaxed.

McEvoy agreed that the subject's arm could have been broken painlessly. When the grips were ended, the subject seated himself calmly and said he had felt nothing.

The experimenter then instructed the subject to return the feeling to his arms. He did so, and immediately doubled over with pain, and gripped his arms in agony, and moaned. He kept this up for several minutes, and it was apparent that severe sprains had been inflicted.

The experimenter then told him to remove all the pain. The subject did so completely in about ten seconds. Although he remained for more than an hour for experimentation and discussion, he paid no attention to his arms, and when he left he reported that he felt excellent.

The subject was again seen three weeks later, and he reported that the pain had at no time returned. What had probably happened was that the injuries had left in the natural course of events. Such residual pain as would have ordinarily remained after several weeks of healing would probably have been liberated if he had been asked to "unlock" the anaesthesia. I would guess that because of the anaesthesia, the traumata had healed faster than they would have ordinarily. This portion of the experiment demonstrates that if it is at all desirable, the anaesthesias can *thoroughly permeate* the limbs and last for some time. It is my opinion that an auto-induced anaesthesia, just as a hysterical one, can last for years.

The subject was demonstrated to Gene Tunney, former world's heavyweight boxing champion. One of his comments is worthy of attention. He remarked that in the ring he had many times received severe injuries, and had not felt them in the excitement of the fight. This again illustrates what cannot be repeated too often. To speak of the waking state, as opposed to the trance state, does not add much to our knowledge. The phenomena of "hypnosis" are impressive only in their quantity, and in the source and intensity of their control.

An evening was devoted to motion picture studies of the two male subjects. Careful inspection of the film indicates a complete verification of what had been previously noticed—the lack of all overt reactions when no cues were available, and an utter absence of change in blood pressure. The lights and excitement associated with the taking of the motion pictures increased the subjects' basic blood pressure, but all other phenomena remained unchanged.

The following conclusions seem valid:

Results are definitely a function of the interaction of technique and subject. Poor subjects may be transformed into good ones. Whether or not a subject believes he is a good subject has nothing to do with the case. Faith is an extraneous issue. Simple mass procedures applied to soldiers could quickly filter out one of five or at worst one of eight who can quickly be taught to make themselves immune to such sounds and pains as they wish. It is not impossible to imagine battalions of self-anaesthetized soldiers going into battle.

When it is realized that hypnosis is nothing more than conditioning, it can be used to produce whatever results may be desired. It is possible to produce all of the phenomena of hypnosis with the subject in complete auto-control and in a waking state at all times.

J. B. S. Haldane has expressed it well.[2] "Anyone who has seen even a single example of the power of hypnotism and suggestion must realize that the face of the world and the possibilities of existence will be totally altered when we can control their effects and standardize their application, as has been possible, for example, with drugs which were once regarded as equally magical."

CHAPTER FIVE

THREE TECHNIQUES OF
AUTOHYPNOSIS*

THERE remains one aspect of hypnosis which, so far, has been untouched by modern experimental techniques. That uninvestigated area is autohypnosis.‡

By autohypnosis is meant the ability to induce, *upon oneself*, the trance of sleeping hypnosis together with such of its phenomena as may be desired. Included are catalepsies, anaesthesias, and amnesias (both in the trance and post-hypnotically) and the varied post-hypnotic suggestions, including positive and negative hallucinations—in short, all the classic phenomena. In autohypnosis not only does the "subject" hypnotize himself and administer the suggestions to himself, but he also has complete control of the trance state at all times. To use a word that should be obsolete, the only person with *rapport* is the subject, and that *rapport* is with himself.

* This chapter originally appeared in *The Journal of General Psychology*, 1941, 24: 423-438.

‡ Wells' work on "waking hypnosis" did not deal with "the production of a sleeping or even a drowsy state." To quote him,[1] his concept of autohypnosis is made clearer when he says, "The step to effective autosuggestion, or autohypnosis, is shorter from waking than from sleeping hypnosis." We can identify his "waking hypnosis" with what we might term *advanced waking suggestion*.

I should like here to record my debt to the work of Clark L. Hull, W. R. Wells, and Paul Campbell Young, and in particular to the first mentioned.

So much for what autohypnosis is. Now let us see what it is not.

It is not the same as the self-hypnosis often mentioned in considering the persistence of symptoms in hysteria; nor is this definition of autohypnosis quite identical with autosuggestion, for the latter is a waking phenomenon and the former involves a trance state. As for the possible identity of autohypnosis with the "samadhic (trance) state of yoga," Behanan[2] has said of hypnosis that "It would be mere speculation of doubtful value either to affirm or deny that the two are essentially similar." This possibility will receive consideration later. Autohypnosis, then, as used herein, is the same as the customary sleeping hypnosis, except that the trance is induced by the "subject" upon himself, and only the "subject" retains complete control of the trance.

Such a condition is of the greatest psychological interest. It is the basic purpose of this paper to present three techniques of autohypnosis in such detail as to make them available to those wishing to do research in this field, and only incidentally to touch upon some of the uses and possible theoretical implications of the techniques.

The first method of autohypnosis may seem obvious, yet I have not encountered its equivalent in the literature. Briefly, we may term it autohypnosis by post-hypnotic suggestion.

In using this technique I find out if the person who wishes to learn autohypnosis is a good hypnotic subject in the first place. I try the usual sleeping hypnosis on the potential subject. If I can produce any limb catalepsies or a glove anaesthesia, or better—and by better I mean a "depth score" of 13 or higher on the scale of Davis and Husband[3]—I find that it is then possible to teach autohypnosis with distinct value to the subject. I consider a limb catalepsy of some sort, or inability to get out of the chair, as a *sine qua non* of the trance before I make any endeavor to teach autohypnosis.

I tell the subject, *who is wide-awake,* and has previously been developed into as good a hypnotic subject as possible, that if he wishes, he can be taught to put himself into a trance wherein he can give himself suggestions exactly as I would give them, and with the same effect, if not better. "We might say," I declare jokingly, "that you can be your own Svengali and Trilby simultaneously." (This expression always appeals to subjects.)

After a discussion of the uses that the subject can make of self-induced post-hypnotic suggestion (else why autohypnosis?) I proceed to emphasize that post-hypnotic suggestions are very effective. I cite instances involving the subject, and tell him that in a few minutes I will hypnotize him and while in the trance I will give him a post-hypnotic suggestion dealing with hypnosis.

I will tell you that whenever you wish to hypnotize yourself, you have merely to sit or lie down as comfortably as you can at the moment, and let the thought flash through your mind that you wish to hypnotize yourself. You will take five deep breaths, and on the fifth breath you will be in the deepest possible trance* and then you will give your-

---

* This may be varied by telling the subject, instead, that it will be necessary only to tell himself *"Fast asleep"* five times to "be in the deepest possible trance." Other variations are, of course, possible. The point is that a convenient post-hypnotic suggestion of autohypnosis is given.

self whatever suggestions you wish, and wake up whenever
you want to. Every time you awaken from a trance you will
feel fine—splendid.

Don't worry about waking up. It won't be a problem.
You know that a mother can sleep through a thunder storm,
but the moment her baby stirs in its crib, or utters the slight-
est cry, the mother is wide-awake. Let us simply say that
the mother's subconscious mind, and yours, are never asleep.
The "subconscious" is a debatable matter, but it's a handy
concept here. So you see, if you're in a trance, and anybody
shouts "Fire!" or calls you for any reason, or you *have* to
awaken for any reason—you will awaken. You will have no
trouble at all, as you shall see.

A good part of the pre-trance instruction is given to
mold the subject's future autohypnotic behavior. Young
has a splendid discussion of the effect of pre-trance
instruction on trance behavior. I have been guided by
his results, and I agree with him that "a genuine hypnosis can exist without the semblance of rapport."[4] I shall
prove this of autohypnosis later.

After these "pre-trance" instructions I have the subject stand up and I demonstrate the "you're falling forward" waking suggestion technique. It works quickly.
I then tell the subject to repeat the "falling forward"
suggestions to himself, without speaking. "*Just say them
mentally, and I'll catch you as you fall forward.*" The
subject gives himself the "falling forward" autosugges-
tions, and I catch him as he falls forward.

"You see," I explain. "It doesn't make any difference *who*
gives you the suggestions. They work, if you want them to
work, and such will be the case when you hypnotize yourself. The source of the suggestions doesn't matter. They may
come from within or without. As long as you coöperate, with

me or with yourself, the suggestions work. And that's the way it will be when you hypnotize yourself. Is everything clear?"

Here the subject often asks one or more of three questions: (*a*) Will I be able to wake myself easily? (*b*) Should I talk to myself in the trance to give myself the suggestions, or should I just think them? (*c*) Will the suggestions I give myself be as effective as the ones you gave me?

To show how easy it is to wake up oneself I re-explain the analogy of the sleeping mother and child, and conclude therefrom that anything that *should* awaken the subject, *will* awaken him.* I emphasize, in addition, that the only one in "rapport" with the subject will be the subject himself. Consequently, whenever he wants to awaken it will be no problem at all because of his "self-rapport."

"Should I talk to myself in the trance to give myself the suggestions, or should I just think them?"

I tell the subject to "think them," that is, to repeat the suggestions mentally. I always tell the subject that parrot-like mimicry of my suggestions is not essential, but that following the general basis and outline of the post-hypnotic suggestions is what matters. I usually give the subject written post-hypnotic suggestions, which he inspects in his waking state whenever he later wishes to practice autohypnosis.

* One of my subjects, the top-ranking student in the art school of a large Eastern college, hypnotizes herself as she rides to school from the suburbs in a trolley car each morning. When somebody calls her by name she awakens instantly and usually hears, *"Oh, you're sleeping. Where were you last night?"* She never misses her corner.

It cannot be emphasized too much that there is no difficulty or shock of any sort when an autohypnotized person "must" awaken.

As for whether autohypnotic suggestions are as effective as what we might call "heterohypnotic" suggestion, I tell the subject that autohypnotic suggestion is at least as good as, or better than, the usual hypnotic suggestion. In the latter, I explain, suggestion comes from the outside, and works on the subject because of his desire to coöperate. In autohypnosis the immediate source of the ideas is "within" the subject, and surely a person will coöperate with himself. The subject's attention is called to his behavior in the "falling forward" demonstration, and I reiterate that the source of the ideas is immaterial, as long as the subject wishes to follow them. The subject is told that, if anything, a well-organized autohypnotic suggestion should work on him more than a "heterohypnotic" one, for the *rapport* of autohypnosis is as complete as can ever be possible. (Remember that up to this point the subject is in a full normal waking state.)

After answering the subject's questions, and making sure that he is at ease, I hypnotize him and tell him all that I have just told him, save in more detail should I consider it necessary. In addition I tell the subject that he will be able to talk to me when he later enters his self-induced trance. I particularly emphasize this suggestion about being able to talk to me while he is in his autohypnotic trance, because I wish to guide the subject and to preclude the faint possibility of my not having *rapport* if the subject were to misunderstand my instructions.

The entire procedure thus far described takes much less time to go through than might at first seem necessary. Twenty minutes is ample. This includes everything so far described, starting with my statement to the subject *"that in a few minutes I will hypnotize him and while in the trance I will give him a post-hypnotic suggestion dealing with hypnosis."*

I awaken the subject and inquire whether there is an amnesia for the trance. This is desirable, but not essential. The subject's answer may usually be guessed by the extent of the amnesia in previous trances. Even with a somewhat poor subject, I find that appropriate training can teach a fairly surprising amount of amnesia, superficially at least. In any event, if the subject seems to remember something, I give some indirect waking suggestion along the lines:

"Yes, of course. You'll forget it. You know how it is with a dream. We forget it a few moments after we awaken," etc.

"Let's take a rest," I then tell the subject. I engage him in conversation about some news item, or any other matter that seems apart from psychology. After no more than five minutes of such discussion, I say something like, "Well. I gave you some instructions about how to hypnotize yourself. Let's see you practice them. You don't even have to try. It will just happen. Five deep breaths, and then you're in a real trance. Come on."

The subject usually smiles and says, "I'll try," or "Here's hoping."

"Go ahead," I say.

The subject takes five breaths (they are often not very deep), his eyes close and he remains quiet.* I let him sit quietly for about a half minute.

"You are fast asleep, aren't you?" I say.

"Yes," is the answer in the usual low voice.

* If the subject does not fall asleep very easily, as he breathes I say *"Fast asleep,"* several times. This suffices but is seldom necessary.

From here on the procedure varies. I usually ask the subject to make a glove or whole arm anaesthesia. *"Let me see you make your right arm anaesthetic,"* I say, *"and tell me when you're ready."*

When careful investigation shows an anaesthesia, at least overtly to me and covertly by the subject's report, it may be taken for granted that all will be well. I have the subject restore sensation to his arm, and tell him to give himself suggestions about his studying (or finger-nails, or piano-playing, or whatever the problem is).

"Use as much of my general language as you can recall. Just think those suggestions with all your might for about (say) five minutes, and tell me when you're ready."

In about that time, more or less (there are never any miracles of accentuated perception of time intervals in hypnosis), the subject says he is ready. *"Very well,"* I say. *"Wake up when you decide to—say in a few minutes."* I give some suggestions about permanent waking amnesias for the trance states and that the subject will always feel splendid on awakening.

Soon the subject opens his eyes and looks around. He is wide awake, and feels fine.

A subject with whom anaesthesias could not be "heterohypnotically" produced would be told in his first autohypnotic trance to produce other effects upon himself which previous experience had shown could be produced by the experimenter. Simple kinaesthetic suggestions will do. The more impressive the effect, the better.

In any case, whether or not anaesthesias can be produced in the trance, if the subject seems to have a slight difficulty in awakening, I say, *"Come on. You can wake up. You're the boss. You're in control. Wake up."* These directions, self-contradictory as they are, will suffice. It will be noted how even these directions stress the subject's autohypnotic control.

We shall consider two other methods of autohypnosis before entering upon a general discussion of all three methods. This procedure will be most conducive to clarity and brevity.

In the autohypnotic method just described it will be recalled that there was frequent mention of the fact that to the subject it does not matter whether the suggestions he gets come from "within" as autosuggestion, or from "without" as heterosuggestion. (I am using the terms auto- and heterosuggestion in the broadest possible sense, to include all ramifications of waking and trance phenomena.)

If such is the case, what would happen if a good hypnotic subject were given the pre-trance preparation described before, with the exception that he would not receive instructions regarding the acquisition of autohypnotic control through post-hypnotic suggestion, nor would he be given such related suggestions hypnotically? I think that it may be agreed that the result would be the same originally good hypnotic subject, who would now be fairly well informed (and *convinced*) about the theory and operational truths of hypnosis.

It is such a "well informed (and *convinced*)" subject that we need for the second technique of autohypnosis. Remember that the first or post-hypnotic method will not be used with this subject.

I give such a subject some typed autohypnotic material which parallels the "heterohypnotic" suggestions

I have previously found effective with him. There is no point in giving a complete verbatim example, for the directions vary from case to case. The illustrative material that follows is composed of a few typical cross-sections of what the subject is instructed to memorize at home, at leisure, and while wide-awake. It reads, in part, something like this:

I feel very comfortable. My arms are so relaxed. My feet feel very relaxed and heavy. I feel so very comfortable and relaxed. My whole body feels comfortable and relaxed. I just want to sleep. I feel so comfortable.

My eyes are getting heavy, so very heavy. They're closing bit by bit, they feel so heavy and relaxed. I feel them closing more and more. I want to sleep, and I want my eyes to close.

These instructions continue and should be adjusted to the subject. It will be noted that the instructions to be memorized are tantamount to the usual hypnotic directions. Toward the end the instructions read:

Now I am fast asleep, in the deepest possible hypnotic sleep. I am in a deep sleep, as deep as the deepest hypnotic sleep I have ever been in. I have complete autohypnotic control of myself. I can give myself autohypnotic suggestions and awaken whenever I wish. I can talk to the person who gave me these autohypnotic instructions, yet I will still remain fast asleep. I will follow such instructions as he gives me, yet I shall still have autohypnotic control.

The subject is told to memorize these instructions, and not to concentrate too much on their meaning. He is told that he may paraphrase them if he wishes. The subject is told not to try to hypnotize himself with these instructions until we have gone over them together, and I have shown him how to use them.

When the subject tells me that he has memorized the instructions, or their essence, I sit him down in a comfortable chair, and tell him that now he can hypnotize himself.

There is no such thing as *A* hypnotizing *B*. All that *A* does is to tell *B* which roads to follow to get to his destination—hypnosis. It doesn't matter who tells you what roads to follow—whether I tell you these roads (or directions), or whether you tell yourself those roads. In any case, if you *follow* those roads, you will hypnotize yourself.

I then repeat most of the pre-trance instructions and demonstrations mentioned in connection with the first method, with the exceptions as previously noted. I explain the concept of an ideomotor act, and I tell him that he has memorized a series of ideomotor acts in his autohypnotic series of directions. This is further explained, and then the subject is told that as he repeats the autohypnotic directions, and puts his entire heart into them, he will find them having effect on him—just as I previously hypnotized him with similar ideomotor suggestions. I answer such questions as the subject may have.

The memorized instructions may be said slowly by the subject in a low voice, or repeated mentally. The former is desirable at first (for the experimenter's sake) if the subject so prefers it, but either will do. It may be necessary to have the subject go through the memorized suggestions three or four times, or more, in order to show the subject the most efficacious way to give himself the suggestions. The experimenter may even help the subject along with some heterosuggestion when the subject seems to need an extra push, but this can be kept to a minimum.

In a short while it will be found that the subject can put himself in an autohypnotic trance. Once he is in the trance, the method proceeds essentially as Method 1, with such differences as are obvious. With practice, the subject can quickly put himself into a trance whenever he wishes. As time goes on the autohypnotic material he thinks (or mumbles) may become more abbreviated, and after a half dozen or more spaced trances the subject finds that he has to spend very little time to get into a trance. A few cursory thoughts about hypnotizing himself will suffice to produce a deep trance, for practice effects are very marked. This will all be considered in my discussion.

We come now to the third and last method of autohypnosis, which method is probably the most fundamental of the three. This might be termed "fractional autohypnosis." Hull[5] in discussing "susceptibility to prestige suggestion" says:

> The essence [of hypnosis] lies in the experimental fact of a quantitative *shift* in the upward direction which may result from the hypnotic procedure. So far as the writer can see, this quantitative phenomenon alone remains of the once imposing aggregate known by the name of hypnosis. But this undoubted fact is quite sufficient to give significance and value to the term.

I should like now to present a method of autohypnosis whereby this "quantitative *shift*" of suggestibility in an upward direction may be induced without the usual hypnotic procedure. It may be compared, in a sense, to the part method in learning, that is, the trance state will be assumed as being composed of discrete parts, each of which will be taught to the potential subject. This analogy will not be followed implicitly, but it gives a good idea of the method.

For this method we need a person with whom it has been found possible to produce, by waking suggestion, some limb catalepsy or an inability to get out of the chair. These qualifications are not at all stringent, and surely not for experimentation. (I shall have more to say later in regard to the selection and percentage of subjects in any of the methods of autohypnosis.)

Once such a potential subject has been selected, the "you're falling forward" waking suggestion technique is demonstrated with him. The subject is then taught to "autosuggest" the falling forward. Some time is spent on this, and in emphasizing that "it doesn't matter *who* gives you the suggestions," as has been described in Method 1.

After the subject has been taught to produce quickly the falling forward postural technique upon himself, and the implications of it have been *hammered* home upon him, a similar demonstration is given of Chevreul's pendulum. No "magnetic" bar is used, and the subject is given waking suggestion that "it's going back and forth, back and forth, like a pendulum," etc. The pendulum is then made to go "round and round." All this, of course, works. The subject then produces the same results upon himself through autosuggestion. This is practiced until the subject, through autosuggestion, can *quickly* produce substantial swinging of the pendulum —both "back and forth" and "round and round."

The subject, in working with Chevreul's pendulum,

has been seated in a comfortable armchair. Waking suggestion is now given that the subject's "right arm feels very heavy," etc. This is kept up for some minutes —say five—and the subject will report that his right hand feels very heavy. Some subjects will be unable to move their right hand. (Such subjects will prove to be splendid for other more advanced phenomena.) In any case, the subject is then taught to autosuggest the heaviness of the right hand. In a short while the subject can do this quickly. A similar procedure is followed, separately, with the left hand, the right leg and then the left leg, that is, heterosuggestion in the waking state is followed by intensive autosuggestion. Then the subject is drilled until, by autosuggestion, he can make either hand or foot very heavy in a short while. This may be done by calling out one extremity after another at random.

A similar procedure is used now to produce heaviness of the entire body, first by heterosuggestion and then by autosuggestion. The latter is drilled thoroughly. A similar procedure is followed in producing catalepsy of the eyes.

After this effort the subject may often complain of fatigue. Whether the subject does so or not, he is told to autosuggest a comfortable and rested body, and he usually does. If he doesn't, a slight "heterosuggestive" push will. This is enough for a beginning, and the subject is told to go home and practice autosuggesting the different phenomena in different combinations. First both arms simultaneously and then both legs simultaneously. Then the entire body is to feel heavy. After this, the eyes are to be shut tight, and he will be able to open them when he decides to do so. He is told that the purpose of this practice is to teach him to make his entire body feel heavy (or relaxed) in a few moments whenever he decides to do so, and at the same time he is to get a catalepsy of the eyes. Should he feel tired after this practice, he will be able to autosuggest it away.

When I next see the subject I have him demonstrate how quickly he can make his entire body feel heavy (or relaxed) coincident with a self-induced catalepsy of the eyes. The subject can produce this quickly if he has given himself a modicum of practice at home.

When I see that the subject can turn this state on and off, almost like an electric light, I give him some more pre-trance preparation. This time it runs along the following lines:

You see that you are learning autohypnosis. It might be clearer if we called it "auto-concentration," for in a sense that's what autohypnosis is. Your entire mind and body are *concentrated* upon whatever effect you wish to produce, and when your entire organism is focused upon one thing, the results may seem remarkable.* We have utter concentration and no divergence of attention, and that's very important. You know, sometimes you find a scratch or bruise on yourself, and have no recollection of having acquired it. You must have had your attention focused on something else, so to all intents and purposes you had an anaesthesia. Well, by appropriate use of autohypnosis you can produce an anaesthesia on yourself, as you shall see.

Following Wells' analogies[6] I then compare the illusions and hallucinations of hypnosis to normal dreams,

* I grant that this language is in the worst tradition of the inspirational psychologists (?) but it is nevertheless clearer to subjects than would be an explanation in terms of "sensory focalization" and "mental set."

and explain that the amnesia that follows hypnotic sleep is much like the amnesia for one's dreams that usually follows on waking from natural sleep.

After this, I describe a typical heterohypnotic somnambulistic trance and I endeavor to act it out very realistically. If it is possible to demonstrate a good subject, that, of course, is to be preferred. The purpose of all this is to convince the subject that there is nothing extraordinary about hypnosis (or autohypnosis) and by pre-trance learning, direct and indirect, to mold his future trance behavior.

Then heterohypnosis is mixed with autohypnosis, i.e., the subject brings himself into as deep a trance as he can, and the experimenter (having shown the subject that the point of origin of the suggestions is immaterial) produces the different trance effects. After this, the experimenter shows the subject how to produce those effects himself.

Some subjects, from the start, need very little heterohypnotic aid before they can produce deep trance phenomena autohypnotically. I advise the experimenter to be careful in his efforts to induce anaesthesias, for when such attempts fail, the subject's confidence is particularly weakened. For that matter, of course, a subject's confidence is weakened by any suggestion that fails.

I remind all of my subjects that aches and pains are warning signals of something wrong with the body. Consequently, they should be careful not to misuse their autohypnotic ability so as to mask physical ailments, and since they probably cannot diagnose their ailments —aside from temporary fatigue and "nervous headaches"—they should let alone that aspect of autohypnosis, as a general rule.

Usually a five minute trance is sufficient time for a subject to give himself autohypnotic post-hypnotic suggestions. A longer period can only help, and is often desirable. Most subjects find that the best time for such suggestions is the morning, a short while after awakening, but this has its exceptions.

We have seen three techniques of autohypnosis. The first and second methods begin by choosing desirable subjects through heterohypnosis, and the third method begins by finding appropriate subjects through simple waking suggestion. Thereafter autohypnosis is taught by: (a) Method 1—post-hypnotic suggestion; (b) Method 2—memorized trance instructions; (c) Method 3—fractional autohypnosis, i.e., the elements of the trance are taught part by part. In each method the character of the pre-trance instructions and demonstrations is important.

These techniques were developed through heterohypnotic work, spaced over two years, with approximately 150 subjects, and through autohypnotic work from an essentially clinical point of view with close to 40 selected cases. At least 20 more subjects, who varied in age from 18 to 30, were used in non-therapeutic autohypnotic experimentation.

May I present a caution. There is no reason, save for experimental purposes, to teach autohypnosis so thoroughly to a good subject that he can produce positive or negative visual and auditory hallucinations. If autohypnosis is taught so thoroughly, it is good policy to give the subject heterohypnotic suggestions that block such autohypnotic hallucinations completely, otherwise you may have a worried subject on your hands.

There are some definite advantages attached to auto-hypnosis. Hull[7] says:

The general nature and proportions of the curve of dimi-nution of [the durability of post-hypnotic suggestion] with the passage of time have become of special significance in [clinical practice] because it has been found that striking improvements in symptoms observable during the trance too often disappear disappointingly soon after its termina-tion, and in spite of the use of vigorous post-hypnotic sug-gestion.

Autohypnosis completely surmounts this diminution of post-hypnotic suggestion. The subject administers the post-hypnotic suggestions to himself whenever he so desires and what in heterohypnosis would be a re-mission of symptoms becomes a self-controlled and periodically reinforced remission.

The important advantage of autohypnosis lies in its ability to overcome the diminution of the effects of post-hypnotic suggestion. For example—one of my cases, a stutterer, treated heterohypnotically, would speak im-peccably for about two days, and then relapse to her old level. With autohypnosis she has no occasion to revisit me. The fundamental reasons for her stuttering were fairly clear, and were fixed, and not variable fac-tors at the time.

There is another advantage to autohypnosis. It means a good deal to a subject not to have to revisit persistently the psychologist for frequent hypnotic aid, whether it be for the problem under treatment or in another connection.

The most impressive thing about the therapeutic use of autohypnosis is the rapidity with which it weakens the feeling of dependency upon the psychologist held by most cases under treatment. True enough, the psychologist temporarily remains the subject's guide, but what is important is that the subject soon realizes that it is only he himself who will do the real work of the cure. In some instances, what the subject is instructed to do with his autohypnotic ability is expected to help him only slightly, but the concepts that he absorbs serve to gain his whole-hearted coöperation in following out the (non-hypnotic) courses of action which may be the real crux of the therapy.

I have used autohypnosis with success in cases of stuttering, nail-biting, anaesthesia for dental use, insomnia, smoking, and the "will to diet." I have been especially interested in teaching it to people who wish to inculcate the "work urge" in themselves. Acting, music, and the "will to write" have been the customary fields here. The results in acting have been quite gratifying, because it seems possible to break completely any trace of self-consciousness.

Practice effects occur, no matter by which method autohypnosis is taught. After a few autohypnotic trances, induced by the subject without any heterohypnotic aid, a minute becomes ample time for the self-induction of the trance, and often a half-minute suffices. Practice effects always occur in heterohypnotic work, so this is no exception, save that the effects seem more marked.

As far as the question of *rapport* is concerned, it seems fair to conclude that there is no *rapport* in autohypnosis, unless it is grafted on the subject in the early stages of teaching autohypnosis. It is true, however, that the subject can voluntarily grant this *rapport* or withhold it in his latter trances. The use of the word *rapport* in this connection is convenient, and for that reason I am using it.

I have not found anything in my work with autohypnosis that conflicts with the "Interpretations" of Hull[8] in regard to heterohypnosis. Particularly would I like to emphasize his point that it really makes no difference to the subject if the suggestions come from within or without. (See especially Hull's section "Ideomotor Action and Monoideism Conceived as Habit Phenomena."[9])

It is my impression, subjective of course, that the distributions of subjects who go to various depths in autohypnosis would not differ significantly from those usually found in heterohypnotic work. Davis and Husband[10] present a fine scale and typical results. Since my techniques were constantly changing until I developed the present methods, distributions that I could present would be fallacious. I have found, however, that at least one of five, and no more than two out of five adults can be taught autohypnosis so thoroughly that they will be able to produce upon themselves the whole gamut of hypnotic phenomena as enumerated in the scoring system of Davis and Husband. The figure is probably closer to one out of five.

This means that it is possible to teach at least one out

of five people to produce, autohypnotically, extensive anaesthesias and catalepsies, and positive and negative visual and auditory hallucinations—particularly positive ones. This can all be done heterohypnotically, but when it is done autohypnotically it brings to mind a question. What about the possible identity of autohypnosis with the trance state of yoga? I cannot answer this except to say that the autohypnotic techniques here presented can probably provide an answer to this question.

This may be relevant. A subject of mine was seated in an ice cream parlor, and spoke of his ability to induce anaesthesia upon himself. (I had been doing some experimental work with him.) To convince his skeptical listeners and to win a bet, he put himself into a trance, gave himself a post-hypnotic anaesthesia of his left hand, and told himself that he would not feel the residual pain when he later told himself, in a waking state, to "shut off" the post-hypnotic anaesthetic suggestion. Everything worked perfectly. I might add that the pain stimulus was a lighted cigarette. The burn healed without any trouble, except some pain a few days later, which some autohypnotic suggestion blocked.

It is true that autohypnotic anaesthesias and catalepsies do not equal the *samadhic* (trance) state of yoga, except, perhaps, on the vaudeville stage. "Sensory withdrawal" is a rather important element. A good autohypnotic subject who tells himself, in a trance, that *nothing whatever* will disturb his trance for the next five minutes seems to have a startlingly complete "sensory withdrawal." It is essential that the subject clearly understand the condition he is to produce upon himself.

In closing, I should like to point out some additional

problems that could be investigated with fruitful results.

1. A large group, naïve and untested to waking suggestion and hypnosis, should be given trance instructions to memorize. How many would learn autohypnosis? How deep would different subjects go?

2. A large group should be given trance instructions to memorize *after* elaborate explanation and demonstration of waking suggestion and hetero- and autohypnosis. How many would learn autohypnosis? How deep would they go?

3. An effort should be made to teach a large group "fractional hypnosis," i.e., teaching the elements of the trance part by part without first picking the better subjects through preliminary waking suggestion. What would the results be?

4. What are the minimum elements that need be explained and demonstrated to prepare a subject for autohypnosis?

5. What connection, if any, is there between autohypnosis and progressive relaxation?

6. To what extent can autohypnotic subjects be trained to get their results in a waking state by their own post-hypnotic suggestion, and thus obviate the necessity for their trances?

7. A careful investigation of positive and negative visual and auditory hallucinations (autohypnotically produced) might throw some light on aspects of imagination. The positive hallucinations, rather than the negative ones, might yield the more significant data.

CHAPTER SIX

THE AGE OF
CONDITIONING

*First they tell you you're wrong, and they can
prove it. Then they tell you you're right, but
it's not important. Then they tell you it's important, but they've known it for years.*
CHARLES F. KETTERING

T HAT is the usual fate of scientific ideas, and why
should mine be exempt? One scholar wrote a book with
a bibliography of 508 references, and took the position
that hypnosis is conditioning—*but*—and hypnosis is conditioning—*except that.*[1] Even more noteworthy was the
man who wrote a two-volume book on hypnosis, and
included the same experiments I had cited four years
earlier. Also overlooking my work completely, he wrote,

"While the conditioned reflex theory is an intensely interesting one, and while it undoubtedly accounts for physical reactions and even for certain complex psychologic
reactions during hypnosis, it does not seem to explain many
important and complex phenomena of the hypnotic state.
In itself, it is not a complete answer. . . ."[2]

And to complete that answer he supplements it with
his thoughts on "oral, anal, and phallic" organ functions.[3]

More comes to mind about these cases of bibliograpic

myopia, but before discussing them further, I shall quote Critchley,[4] the eminent English neurologist:

"The bibliography should always be scrutinized with meticulous care. What you have to say has probably been said years before, perhaps many times before, and almost certainly in more graceful prose."

Now, skipping over any comments on his prose, I shall proceed to a consideration of the work of Theodore Barber,[5] for the theory of hypnosis currently in the ascendence is identified with him.

Essentially this theory has two parts. The first is that *all*—repeat, *all*—hypnotic phenomena are possible in the waking state—anaesthesias, hallucinations, post-hypnotic suggestions, "hypnotic crimes"—everything. The evidence for this belief is strong, but as I shall show, it suffers from critical deficiencies.

The second aspect of this theory is that hypnosis is essentially a matter of motivation, expectation, and preconception. A sort of placebo effect. Hypnosis happens, is the belief, because the subject expects it to happen. To Barber, then, hypnosis is really a problem in social psychology. In more technical terms, this theory considers hypnosis a matter of cognitive expectancy and "instructional-situational variables."

This theory, we will recall, is a reincarnation of the much earlier theories of Rosenow,[6] Lundholm,[7] Pattie,[8] Dorcus,[9] and White[10] discussed on page 23 of this very book. But Barber mentions only Pattie, three lines in passing.

"The formulation," writes Barber, "to be presented in this text differs radically from almost all previous formulations [Sarbin excepted, 1950] in that it views the construct 'hypnosis' (or 'hypnotic state' or 'trance') as unnecessary and misleading."[11]

The fact is that when Barber was still a teenager, the earlier editions of *What Is Hypnosis* appeared, saying such (then) revolutionary things as:

"This . . . cannot be repeated too often. To speak of the waking state, as opposed to the trance state, does not add much to our knowledge.[12] Although almost everybody believes that the *trance* is a fundamental phenomenon of hypnosis, there is now little support for this opinion. . . . The truth is that the trance is not at all important.[13] . . . the waking and the trance states . . . are not differentiated by physiological processes, thinking included.[14] As we have seen, 'hypnosis' and 'trance' are terms of convenience which have become attached to aspects of conditioning."[15]

What Is Hypnosis was also the first publication to use the construction, "the subject was conditioned to, etc.," as a synonym for giving a subject a suggestion. This usage has since become a standard appurtenance in the literature.

And Barber's omission of the conditioned reflex theory of hypnosis can only befuddle his readers. This theory was first enunciated by Pavlov and fully developed in *What Is Hypnosis*. In the light of our knowledge of verbal conditioning, it is almost pitiable to read in Barber's next to closing paragraph, "Research in 'hypnosis' . . . offers rewarding possibilities for the study of the effects of language (verbal stimulation) on behavior and on physiological processes."[16]

My substantive criticisms of Barber are five in number.

First, motivation and cognitive expectancy are non-sensical as explanations of complex and long-delayed post-hypnotic suggestions. G. H. Estabrooks[17] illustrates this.

"The writer [Estabrooks] recently ran across a case where the posthypnotic suggestion seemed to be fairly strong after twenty years.

"During . . . [World War I] he was interested in the study of hypnotism and was far more inclined to go in for 'stunts' in those early days. He had a favorite trick with one subject. He would say, 'Watch the front.' Whereupon the subject would stand up and shout, 'Call out the guard. Here comes Paul Revere.'

"It happened that recently the operator met this subject and in the course of the conversation suddenly said, 'Watch the front.' The subject looked puzzled, then said, 'Call out the guard. Paul Revere is coming.' Then he immediately looked even more puzzled and added, 'I wonder why I said that. Somehow something you said recalls the last war and all the muck in the trenches. I never recalled the whole thing quite so vividly before.'"

To explain this successfully carried out twenty-year-old post-hypnotic suggestion by Barber's theory is impossible. However, it is easy to explain this from the conditioned reflex point of view.

My second objection to Barber is brief, but extremely critical. Barber omits any mention[18] or consideration of "autohypnosis," "self-hypnosis," and "autosuggestion." This must mean, among other things, that his theoretical structure cannot integrate the many published findings in autohypnosis—including those of this book. As we have seen, autohypnosis fits neatly into firmly established conditioning theory.

Thirdly, Barber found that "Subjects are as suggestible or 'hypnotizable' when the test-suggestions are presented relatively impersonally (e.g., by a tape-recording of the experimenter's voice) as when presented personally (e.g., orally by the experimenter)."[19] And this despite Barber's understandably "strong expectations that suggestibility would be higher with the personal oral presentation. . . ."[20]

This finding presents no mystery to the conditioned reflex theory of hypnosis. If a subject has conditioned verbal bells, you can ring them—whether the words are tape-recorded or larynx-emitted. But Barber is perplexed by his results. There's nothing wrong with his results. The only thing wrong is his theory.

We come now to experimentation with the most devastating implications to the motivation-expectation-cognition believers. Interestingly enough, these findings come from outside the field of hypnotic research, but what is even more interesting is that these findings come from research in conditioning. These studies are quite important in themselves, but they are utterly shattering to the Barber-promulgated theory of cognitive expectancy, and they form *the basis of my fourth objection to Barber's theory.*

Irwin Mandel and Wagner Bridger at the Albert Einstein College of Medicine had been studying how thinking and feeling affect the acquisition and extinction of conditioned reflexes.[21] If you *expect* a shock, will you have a strong emotional reaction even if you don't get the shock? Indeed. And what, for instance, is the emotional difference between getting a *real* shock and "only" getting the *threat* of a shock? Further, how will these two kinds of conditionings fade?

What Mandel and Bridger studied was "cognitive expectancy" (Barber's term): how do the ideas in the head of an experimental subject affect the acquisition and the extinction of a conditioned response—in this case a conditioned galvanic skin reflex to a shock of the hand?

In Mandel's words, "We have been studying the interaction between the manipulation of human cognitions and what have been considered to be the basic laws of learning."[22] Important in general, but particularly critical to the widely promulgated Barber theory.

The findings of Mandel and Bridger can be put in one sentence: *When cognitive expectancy runs counter to conditioning, conditioning wins every time,* "regardless of whether . . . expectations have been left either partially structured . . . or completely unstructured . . . ,"[23] i.e., regardless of whether or not the subject has any pre-conceptions.

"For several years," [Mandel and Bridger reported,[24]] "we have attempted to investigate the relation between human cognitive processes and the laws of classical conditioning. . . . A few investigators . . . avoided either inquiring into or deliberately manipulating subjects' cognitive expectancies. . . .

"In recent years there has been a general resurgence of interest in the role of cognitive processes in human behavior. In the area of classical conditioning research this resurgence has produced a swing of the intellectual pendulum so extreme as to suggest that human conditioned responses are solely a function of cognitive processes. . . ."

[How familiar this sounds! Apparently Barber is not the only culprit.]

"In a general sense we have posed the following questions: . . . If the subjects continue to respond . . . contrary to their cognitive expectancies, do these responses follow the conventional and widely accepted laws of behavior? How can one be sure of what a subject's cognitive expectancies really are? Why should we as researchers expect there to be human behavior that is contrary to human cognitive expectancy?" [Propaganda, history, and hypnosis show us how true this is.]

Mandel and Bridger then say of one of their very important experiments, "This experiment, therefore, served to firmly establish the existence of a conditioned differential galvanic skin reflex that was manifested *contrary to the subject's cognitive expectancy. . . .*" [Italics mine.]

Of another experiment of theirs, they say that their results lend "strong support to the notion that there exists an aspect of human classical conditioning *that is not dependent upon the subject's expectancy* . . . [and] that when cognitive factors are reduced or eliminated, the resulting conditioned response obeys different behavioral laws than when it is under cognitive control." [Italics mine.]

Mandel and Bridger conclude "that the conditioned response may have two aspects: one a function of expectancy, the other independent of expectancy. . . . As a final note, we would like to emphasize that *we do not doubt that cognitive expectancy plays a role in classical conditioning. [But we] have dealt with conditioned responses that not only are not expectancy dependent, but manifest themselves contrary to a cognitive expectancy. . . ."* [Italics mine.]

Even though, at this point, we need no further evidence of the complete bankruptcy of the cognitive expectancy theory of hypnosis, London, Hart, and Leibovitz[25] provide *my fifth and final objection* to Barber's theory. In London's words, "This article reports the first discovery of a relationship between electrical brain wave patterns and hypnotic susceptibility."[26] This is particularly interesting, since earlier research showed no relationship of EEG patterns to hypnotic susceptibility. In this study the good hypnotic subjects had higher durations of alpha rhythms (i.e., 8-13 cycle per second brain waves) than the poorer subjects.

What is important about London, Hart, and Leibovitz is that they demonstrated, for the first time, that hypnotic subjects are physiologically different from non-hypnotic subjects. London's paper verifies the belief of the old stage hypnotists that some people are good subjects and some are not. Svengali was right. Some have got it and some have not. And if they've got it, you can shove your hand right in through their ears and grab their brains.

I might say that Barber's thoughts on hypnotic crimes could easily be checked. Let Barber find me a random group of a hundred males ages twenty-one to twenty five. I would pick three subjects from this group and subject them to a week's worth of hypnotic training in which they would be instructed to shoot Barber (much as in *The Manchurian Candidate*, a book Condon has credited me with inspiring). I would then give Barber one week during which he could exhort these subjects as much as he wanted *in a waking state*. If, in thirty days thereafter, one of my subjects did not try to kill Barber, he could consider his theories of hypnosis verified. I would not be interested in doing this experiment without a waiver from Barber and from all of the appropriate legal jurisdictions.*

We can do in the waking state *almost* everything that can be done in a hypnotic state—*almost* everything, but not quite. And that is all the difference. *Vive la différence!* And the difference varies among individuals according to their personal conditionings.

The residue of hypnosis was well described by Hull. "Its essence lies in the experimental fact of a quantitative *shift* in the upward direction which may result from the hypnotic procedure. So far as the writer can see, this quantitative phenomenon alone remains of the once imposing aggregate known by the name of hypnosis. But this undoubted fact is quite sufficient to give significance and value to the term."[27] Hull said this forty years ago, and his conclusion emerges unscathed despite the great amount of research that has taken place since then.

We all live in private worlds created by our conditionings. People ask, "Can I use hypnotism?" What they mean is, "Do I have conditionings—or brain wave patterns—that can be elicited?" Hypnosis is fundamentally a *recall* process. You have to have it before it can come out. Yet these old conditionings can be used to

* I doubt that this experiment is legally possible. Besides, Ted Barber's work is much too important to terminate or even interrupt. And he's a pleasant luncheon companion, too.

facilitate new ones. Though hypnosis is helpful in manufacturing new responses, fundamentally it is an elicited *old* response.

The issue is no longer hypnosis. With our present knowledge, we can safely say that the real issue is conditioning, and hypnosis is just one of its aspects. I even incline to the opinion that *psychotherapy* is a matter of conditioning, but I have explained this in detail elsewhere.[28]

If we look at the world with our eyes wide open, the conclusion is inescapable: This is the age of conditioning. The psychological principles involved in the manipulation of a single mind have turned out to be just as true applied to the manipulation of hundreds of millions of minds. And the principles are quite simple. Only the media are complicated.

After all, through conditioning methods pigeons have been trained to inspect transistors (William W. Cumming.)[29] Through conditioning, chickens have been taught to play the piano (Keller Breland and his wife, Marian).[30] And Skinner taught pigeons to operate guided missiles. He used three pigeons—two out of three had to agree on the target, so any dissenter could be outvoted ("Pigeons in a Pelican").[31] What can this possibly augur for people?

Fortunately, the conditioned reflex is a stick with two ends. It can be picked up by one end and used to punish us. Or it can be picked up by the other end and used to help us. All that stands in the way of our success is—our old conditionings.

REFERENCES

CHAPTER ONE

FUNDAMENTALS: CONDITIONING AND HYPNOSIS

1. HUXLEY, JULIAN. "The Biologist Looks at Man." *Fortune,* December, 1942, p. 139.
2. PAVLOV, I. P. *Conditioned Reflexes.* Oxford University Press, 1927.
   ——. *Lectures on Conditioned Reflexes.* Vol. I. International Publishers, New York, 1928.
   ——. *Conditioned Reflexes and Psychiatry.* International Publishers, New York, 1941.
3. HUDGINS, C. V. "Conditioning and the Voluntary Control of the Pupillary Light Reflex." *Journal of General Psychology,* 1933, 8: 3-51.
4. MENZIES, R. "Further Studies in Conditioned Vasomotor Responses in Human Subjects." *Journal of Experimental Psychology,* 1941, 29: 457-482.
5. WATSON, J. B. *The Ways of Behaviorism.* Harper and Brothers, New York, 1928, p. 97.
6. PAVLOV, I. P. *Conditioned Reflexes.* Oxford University Press, 1927, p. 407.
7. PAVLOV, I. P. *Conditioned Reflexes and Psychiatry.* International Publishers, New York, 1941, 111-112.
8. BECHTEREV, V. M. *General Principles of Human Reflexology.* International Publishers, New York, translated from the Russian edition of 1928, p. 186.
9. BASS, M. J. "Differentiation of the Hypnotic Trance from Normal Sleep." *Journal of Experimental Psychology,* 1931, 14: 382-399.
10. ELLSON, D. G. "Hallucinations Produced by Sensory

Conditioning." *Journal of Experimental Psychology*, 1941, 28: 1-20.

11. ERICKSON, M. H. "The Induction of Color Blindness by a Technique of Hypnotic Suggestion." *Journal of General Psychology*, 1939, 20: 61-89.

12. BLAKE, H., and GERARD, R. W. "Brain Potentials during Sleep." *American Journal of Physiology*, 1937, 119: 692-703.

13. LOOMIS, A. L., HARVEY, E. N., and HOBART, G. "Brain Potentials during Hypnosis." *Science*, 1936, 83: 239-241.

14. SHAGASS, C. "Conditioning the Human Occipital Alpha Rhythm to a Voluntary Stimulus." *Journal of Experimental Psychology*, 1942, 31: 367-379.

15. LUNDHOLM, H., and LÖWENBACH, H. "Hypnosis and the Alpha Activity of the Electroencephalogram." *Character and Personality*, 1942, 11 No. 2: 145-149.

16. KELLEY, E. L. "An Experimental Attempt to Produce Artificial Chromaesthesia by the Technique of the Conditioned Response." *Journal of Experimental Psychology*, 1934, 17: 315-341.

17. ELLSON, D. G. *Op. cit.*

18. ELLSON, D. G. "Critical Conditions Influencing Sensory Conditioning." *Journal of Experimental Psychology*, 1942, 31: 331-338.

19. PERKY, C. W. "An Experimental Study of Imagination." *American Journal of Psychology*, 1910, 21: 422-452.

20. MILLER, J. G. "Discrimination without Awareness." *American Journal of Psychology*, 1939, 52: 562-578.

21. ROWLAND, L. W. "Will Hypnotized Persons Try to Harm Themselves or Others?" *Journal of Abnormal and Social Psychology*, 1939, 34: 114-117.

22. WELLS, W. R. "Experiments in the Hypnotic Production of Crime." *Journal of Psychology*, 1941, 11: 63-102.

23. BRENMAN, M. "Experiments in the Hypnotic Production of Anti-Social and Self-Injurious Behavior." *Psychiatry*, 1942, 5: 49-61.

CHAPTER TWO

FUNDAMENTALS: HYPNOTIC REACTION
PATTERNS

1. ROSENOW, C. "Meaningful Behavior in Hypnosis." *American Journal of Psychology*, 1928, 40: 205-235.
2. LUNDHOLM, H. "An Experimental Study of Functional Anaesthesias as Induced by Suggestion in Hypnosis." *Journal of Abnormal and Social Psychology*, 1928, 23: 337-355.
3. PATTIE, F. A. "The Genuineness of Hypnotically Produced Anaesthesia on the Skin." *American Journal of Psychology*, 1937, 49: 435-443.
4. DORCUS, R. M. "Modification by Suggestion of Some Vestibular and Visual Responses." *American Journal of Psychology*, 1937, 49: 82-87.
5. WHITE, R. W. "A Preface to the Theory of Hypnotism." *Journal of Abnormal and Social Psychology*, 1941, 36: 477-505.
6. SALTER, A. "Three Techniques of Autohypnosis." *Journal of General Psychology*, 1941, 24: 423-438.
7. BIER, W. "Beitrag zur Beeinflussung des Kreislaufes durch psychische Vorgänge." *Zeitschrift für Klinische Medizin*, 1930, 113: 762-781.
8. LOOMIS, A. L., HARVEY, E. N., and HOBART, G. *Op. cit.*
9. BLAKE, H., and GERARD, R. W. *Op. cit.*
10. NYGARD, J. W. "Cerebral Circulation Prevailing during Sleep and Hypnosis." *Psychological Bulletin*, 1937, 34: 727.
11. FULDE, E. "Über den Einfluss hypnotischer Erregungszustände auf den Gasaustausch." *Zeitschrift für gesamte Neurologie und Psychiatrie*, 1937, 159: 761-766.
12. JENNESS, A., and WIBLE C. L. "Respiration and Heart Action in Sleep and Hypnosis." *Journal of General Psychology*, 1937, 16: 197-222.
13. GOLDWYN, J. "The Effect of Hypnosis on Basal Metabol-

ism." *Archives of Internal Medicine*, 1930, 45: 109-114.

14. BASS, M. J. "Differentiation of the Hypnotic Trance from Normal Sleep." *Journal of Experimental Psychology*, 1931, 14: 382-399.

15. HULL, C. L. *Hypnosis and Suggestibility*. D. Appleton-Century Co., New York, 1933.

16. WHITE, R. W., and SHEVACH, B. J. "Hypnosis and the Concept of Dissociation." *Journal of Abnormal and Social Psychology*, 1942, 37: 309-328.

17. DAVIS, L. W., and HUSBAND, R. W. "A Study of Hypnotic Susceptibility in Relation to Personality Traits." *Journal of Abnormal and Social Psychology*, 1931, 26: 175-182.

18. CARLSON, E. R. "Infantile Cerebral Palsy; Its Treatment by Selective Inhibition of Sensory Stimuli." *Annals of Internal Medicine*, 1937, 324-334.

19. *Personal conversation with the author*, November, 1942.

20. LIVINGOOD, F. G. "Hypnosis as an Aid to Adjustment." *Journal of Psychology*, 1941, 12: 203-207.

21. *Personal communication to the author*, September, 1942.

22. KRASNOGORSKI, N. I. "Conditioned Reflexes in the Psychopathology of Childhood." *American Journal of Diseases of Children*, 1933, 45: 355-370.

23. LLOYD, B. L. *Hypnotism in the Treatment of Disease*. Bale and Danielsson, London, 1934, p. 5.

24. TUCKEY, C. L. *Treatment by Hypnotism and Suggestion*. Baillière, Tindall and Cox, London, 1921, p. 64.

25. WHITE, M. M. "Physical and Mental Traits of Individuals Susceptible to Hypnosis." *Journal of Abnormal and Social Psychology*, 1930, 25: 293-298.

26. DAVIS, L. W., and HUSBAND, R. W. *Op. cit.*

27. HULL, C. L. *Op. cit.*, p. 86.

28. HULL, C. L. *Op. cit.*, pp. 398-399, 150, 347.

29. FREUD, S., and BREUER, J. *Studies in Hysteria*. Nervous and Mental Disease Publishing Co., New York, 1936, p. 203.

30. Freud, S. *Group Psychology and the Analysis of the Ego.* The International Psycho-Analytical Press, London, 1922, pp. 36-37.
31. Freud, S. *Psychoanalysis: Exploring the Hidden Recesses of the Mind.* Translated by A. A. Brill, Encyclopaedia Britannica. Quoted in:
    Brill, A. A. *The Basic Writings of Sigmund Freud.* The Modern Library, New York, 1938, pp. 6-7.
32. Cohen, M. R. *A Preface to Logic.* Henry Holt and Company, New York, 1944, p. 182.
33. Cohen, M. R., and Nagel, E. *An Introduction to Logic and Scientific Method.* Harcourt, Brace and Company, New York, 1936, p. 214.
34. *American Journal of the Medical Sciences.* 1944, 207: 817.
35. *Archives of Neurology and Psychiatry.* 1944, 51: 500.
36. Grotjahn, M. *Psychosomatic Medicine.* 1944, 6: 278.
37. *Archives of Neurology and Psychiatry. Op. cit.*
38. Erickson, M. *Psychiatry.* 1944, 7 No. 2: 195-196.
39. Brenman, M., and Gill, M. M. *Hypnotherapy.* Josiah Macy, Jr. Foundation, 1944, pp. 80-81.
40. Salter, A., *Conditioned Reflex Therapy.* Farrar, Straus & Young, New York, 1949.

CHAPTER THREE

PRELIMINARY EXPERIMENTS IN AUTOHYPNOSIS

1. Salter, A. "Three Techniques of Autohypnosis." *Journal of General Psychology*, 1941, 24: 423-438.

CHAPTER FOUR

A STUDY OF GROUP III

1. Wells, F. L., and Ruesch, J., editors. *Mental Examiners' Handbook.* Psychological Corporation, 1942.
2. Haldane, J. B. S. *Daedalus, or Science and the Future.* E. P. Dutton and Co., 1924, p. 75.

CHAPTER FIVE

THREE TECHNIQUES OF AUTOHYPNOSIS

1. WELLS, W. R. "Experiments in Waking Hypnosis for Instructional Purposes." *Journal of Abnormal and Social Psychology*, 1924, 18: 389-404.
2. BEHANAN, K. T. *Yoga: A Scientific Evaluation.* Macmillan, 1937, p. 237.
3. DAVIS, L. W. and HUSBAND, R. W. "A Study of Hypnotic Susceptibility in Relation to Personality Traits." *Journal of Abnormal and Social Psychology*, 1931, 26: 175-182.
4. YOUNG, P. C. "Is *Rapport* an Essential Characteristic of Hypnosis?" *Journal of Abnormal and Social Psychology*, 1927, 22: 130-139.
5. HULL, C. L. *Hypnosis and Suggestibility.* Appleton-Century, 1933, p. 392.
6. WELLS, W. R. *Op. cit.*, p. 397.
7. HULL, C. L., *Op. Cit.*, p. 156.
8. *Ibid.*, p. 387.
9. *Ibid.*, pp. 398-399.
10. DAVIS, L. W. and HUSBAND, R. W. *Op. cit.*

CHAPTER SIX

THE AGE OF CONDITIONING

1. WEITZENHOFFER, A. M. *Hypnotism.* John Wiley & Sons, Inc., New York, 1953.
2. WOLBERG, L. R. *Medical Hypnosis.* Two volumes. Grune & Stratton, New York, 1948, Vol. I, p. 77.
3. *Ibid,* Vol. I, p. 86.
4. *Neurology.* 1951, Vol. I, No. 6, "Newsletter," p. 1.
5. BARBER, T. X. *Hypnosis.* Van Nostrand Reinhold Co., New York, 1969.

6. Rosenow, C. "Meaningful Behavior in Hypnosis." *Amercan Journal of Psychology,* 1928, 40: 205-235.

7. Lundholm, H. "An Experimental Study of Functional Anaesthesias as Induced by Suggestion in Hypnosis." *Journal of Abnormal and Social Psychology,* 1928, 23: 337-355.

8. Pattie, F. A. "The Genuineness of Hypnotically Produced Anaesthesia of the Skin." *American Journal of Psychology,* 1937, 49: 435-443.

9. Dorcus, R. M. "Modification by Suggestion of Some Vestibular and Visual Responses." *American Journal of Psychology,* 1937, 49: 82-87.

10. White, R. W. "A Preface to the Theory of Hypnotism." *Journal of Abnormal and Social Psychology,* 1941, 36: 477-505.

11. Barber, T. X. Op. cit., p. 7. *See also* p. 221.

12. Salter, A. *What Is Hypnosis.* Richard R. Smith, New York, 1944, p. 55.

13. *Ibid.,* p. 14.

14. *Ibid.,* p. 15.

15. *Ibid.,* p. 26.

16. Barber, T. X. *Op. cit.,* p. 242.

17. Estabrooks, G. H. *Hypnotism.* E. P. Dutton & Co., Inc., New York, 1943, p. 81.

18. Barber, T. X. *Op. cit.,* Index, pp. 279-282.

19. *Ibid.,* pp. 96-97.

20. *Ibid.,* p. 96.

21. Bridger, W. H. and Mandel, I. J. "Cognitive Expectancy and Autonomic Conditioning: Extension of Schizokinesis." *Recent Advances in Biological Psychiatry,* Plenum Press, New York, 1965, 7: 79-83.

———. "A Comparison of GSR Fear Responses Produced by Threat and Electric Shock." *Journal of Psychiatric Research,* 1964, 2: 31-40.

———. "Abolition of the PRE by Instructions in GSR Conditioning." *Journal of Experimental Psychology,* 1965, 69: 476-482.

———. "Interaction between Instructions and ISI in Conditioning and Extinction of the GSR." *Journal of Experimental Psychology,* 1967, 74: 36-43.

———. "Cognitive Factors in GSR Generalization to Verbal Stimuli." *Proceedings,* 75th Annual Convention, APA, 1967, pp. 51-52.

———. "Is There Classical Conditioning Without Cognitive Expectancy?" *Psychophysiology,* in press.

22. *Personal conversation with Mandel,* January, 1970.

23. BRIDGER, W. H. and MANDEL, I. J. *Op. cit.,* APA, 1967.

24. BRIDGER, W. H. and MANDEL, I. J. *Op. cit., Psychophysiology,* in press.

25. LONDON, P., HART, J. T., and LEIBOVITZ, M. P. "EEG Alpha Rhythms and Susceptibility to Hypnosis." *Nature,* 1968, 219: 71-72.

26. LONDON, P. *Behavior Control.* Harper & Row, New York, 1969, p. 226.

27. HULL, C. L. *Hypnosis and Suggestibility.* Appleton-Century-Crofts, New York, 1933, pp. 392-393.

28. SALTER, A. *Conditioned Reflex Therapy.* Revised edition in preparation, Farrar, Straus & Giroux, New York. Capricorn, New York, 1961; Farrar, Straus & Company, New York, 1949.

29. CUMMING, W. W. "A Bird's Eye Glimpse of Men and Machines." *The Control of Human Behavior,* edited by R. E. Ulrich, T. J. Stachnik, and J. H. Mabry; Scott, Foresman & Co., Glenview, Ill., 1966, pp. 246-256.

30. BRELAND, K. and BRELAND, M. "A Field of Applied Animal Psychology." *American Psychologist,* 1951, 6: 202-204.

———. "The Misbehavior of Organisms." *American Psychologist,* 1961, 16: 681-684.

———. *Animal Behavior.* Macmillan, New York, 1966, p. 210.

31. SKINNER, B. F. "Pigeons in a Pelican," *American Psychologist,* 1960, 15: 28-37.

INDEX